BREAK FREE FROM

SUCKVILLE

How a Simple Mental Change Will Spark Your Performance

BREAK FREE FROM

SUCKVILLE

How a Simple Mental Change Will Spark Your Performance

BHRETT McCABE, PhD

606 PUBLISHING

Break Free From Suckville:
How a Simple Mental Change Will Spark Your Performance

Copyright © 2021 by Bhrett McCabe, Ph.D.

All rights reserved. Printed in the United States of America. No part of this book may be used or reproduced in any manner whatsoever without written permission except in the case of brief quotations, embodied in academic or trade publications for purposes of educational dissemination. For additional information, contact 606 Publishing, The MindSide, 1401 Doug Baker Blvd. Suite 107-110, Birmingham, AL 35242.

For more information, please visit:

www.bhrettmccabe.com

contact@themindside.com

FIRST EDITION

Designed by Brett Basham

ISBN: 978-0-9982174-2-0

ACKNOWLEDGEMENTS

To every parent, player, and coach who trusted me to help them achieve their dreams, I cannot express my gratitude enough. It is a great honor to be a guide in your journey.

To my family, I love you. Thank you for the opportunity to chase my dream. I know I have experienced plenty of struggles and lived some time in Suckville, but you stood there with me, giving me the strength to keep going.

"There will be obstacles.

There will be doubters.

There will be mistakes.

But with hard work, there are no limits."

- Michael Phelps

United States Olympic Team – Swimming

Winner of 23 Olympic Gold Medals

PREFACE

The ballpark was scattered with lawn chairs and umbrellas, lining the chain link fences separating the parents from the baseball players. The scene repeated itself across the expansive public park, with parents shouting support to each player on the field.

The coaches in the dugouts were intensely focused on their teams, encouraging each player to enjoy the game and give it all that they had. From the youngest competitors to the oldest high school ballplayers, the game's noise served as a backdrop to the clutter in their heads. If there was only a way to quiet the shouts of encouragement from the well-meaning parents, the players could probably focus better.

"Raise your arms, Johnny," one parent screamed.

"Just throw strikes, Billy," another parent from the opposing team yelled.

"Focus on the pitch!" another parent yelled.

Strike one.

Strike two.

Strike three.

Johnny struck out and slowly walked back to the dugout. His coach tapped him on the shoulder and offered some simple words of encouragement, but it was not the time for that. His dad met him in the dugout, speaking through the chain link fence, reminding him to do what they had worked on last night in the batting cage in their backyard. Johnny just looked down at the ground. He was overwhelmed and frustrated. When he worked on hitting at night with his dad, he was so good. If he continued to struggle, there would be no chance to play in college. As a senior in high school, he was falling behind other players.

His mind was cluttered with mechanics, expectations, and hope with each at-bat in a real game. All he wanted was to find the freedom he had as a hitter just three years ago. As a rising freshman in high school, he was an All-Star, traveling the country and dominating the opposition.

The pressure was intense, even though it was self-inflicted. But that type of pressure is probably the hardest to deal with for players at every level of the game. When self-doubt, frustration, and anger build, a perfect storm starts swirling. There is nothing you can do to avoid the pain that follows.

For a player like Johnny, every opportunity to break free from the struggles and frustration becomes nothing more than a reminder of what once was possible. Words of encouragement and support do nothing but create more frustration.

"I should be better than this!"

"I just want to enjoy the game again!"

"Why do they have it easier than me!"

Those thoughts become the norm. But it does not have to be that way.

Any competition has the potential to go against you, facing defeat right up until the final play, out, or hole are completed. There will never be a time in sports where the outcome is easily determined or achicvable. It takes risk, and it requires you to fight through the buildup of struggles that surround you.

Johnny is every player who has played any sport on the planet. Johnny is also everyone who has ever wanted something but had to deal with the struggles and frustrations of achievement.

Struggle is an equal opportunity offender and takes no prisoners. It may be harsh, but it is never fatal. While Johnny, you, and I have all struggled with confidence at times in our lives, the truth is you have endured far greater and will continue to find ways to succeed in the shadows of struggle. It is never the mere presence of difficulty that causes the problems, but instead, your mental framework tries to understand why it is happening and what it means about you. The "Why" and "What" are where the trouble starts.

Your lowest points reveal your greatest strengths. When doubt is the most intense, determination finds a way to keep you moving. When fear builds, faith must take hold.

No matter what you are going through competitively, you will emerge greater than who entered the fray. What that takes is a change of perspective. It is time YOU start fighting for yourself.

You are responsible for the power of your mindset. No one has the right to control your opinions or destroy your belief and confidence. You must remind yourself why you are worthy of your success and begin to build the positive momentum to succeed. It is time you start fighting for yourself.

CONTENTS

INTRODUCTION

In front of a live audience of 20,000 devoted fans and millions more on live television, Kurt Warner shared the secrets to his success. As a newly inducted member of the National Football League's Pro Football Hall of Fame, Warner had an unconventional journey to becoming one of the league's all-time greats. A story of perseverance and resilience overshadowed by record-breaking touchdowns and dramatic victories.

Warner burst onto the national scene as a member of the Los Angeles Rams when the starter, Trent Green, suffered a season-ending knee injury during the preseason. Warner was not a top prospect or a seasoned veteran. Instead, he was a former grocery store clerk who sharpened his skills in the Arena Football League, where football games are played inside on hockey rink-sized fields with unconventional rules. Players rising from the Arena Football League do not traditionally become starting quarterbacks in the NFL, much less a Hall of Fame quarterback. Warner is not the norm.

In his first season as the starting quarterback, Warner took over the NFL, setting passing records as the leader of the "greatest show on turf," a nickname for his fast-paced, dynamic offense. The Los Angeles Rams defeated the Tennessee Titans in Super Bowl XXXIV and etched their collective names in history and football lore. Warner was the Super Bowl MVP and became a household name in what seemed to be an overnight success. Yet, it was many sleepless nights for that overnight success.

Warner had the size and tools to be a quarterback in the NFL, by theory. But he did not even start or play for his college team for four years. The story rivaled Tom Brady, one that fans of the NFL have admired for Brady's longevity, durability, and success. Still, while Brady waited his turn at the University of Michigan, Warner did so at the University of Northern Iowa. To be honest, there could not be a more significant difference between the two college football programs.

The University of Michigan is a national powerhouse, perennially one of the largest financial budgets in college football. Northern Iowa plays in a lower classification and the shadows of The University of Iowa and Iowa State University. Warner had been cut or released by nearly every professional franchise he had played for and pondered if he would ever reach his potential, playing in the NFL.

Warner had the physical size and arm strength, but something was missing. He kept getting chances, albeit small ones, but he never progressed in the league. Well, until he did.

In his speech to the Hall of Fame audience, Warner shared some insight into this untraditional journey:

- He considered transferring many times in college because he could not find a way to get on the field.
- He worked nights stocking shelves at a grocery store to pay the bills while he trained during the day for an uncertain, potential tryout in the future.
- He was afraid of being tackled in high school, a challenging fear since he played tackle football.
- He admitted he was "crippled" by the fear of the unknown, an uncertain future.
- He was cut from his first NFL team, left with no money for gas to drive his family home, and he had to convince a gas attendant to give him some gas.
- Five years later, twelve teams passed on an opportunity to sign

in for a tryout, but he went to the 13th team – the St. Louis Rams and legendary coach Dick Vermeil.

- The final cuts with the St. Louis Rams came down to a coach taking a chance on him as the 3rd team quarterback. It was a risky roster decision because, during his first season, he only played a handful of snaps.

You can learn a lot from reading the transcripts of interviews and Hall of Fame induction speeches. Warner did not have it easy and was certainly not a "can't miss" prospect.

Warner is not much different than you. He experienced periods of significant doubt and frustration of not meeting his potential. His journey never followed a traditional route, which made him even more unsure of a future in professional football. While he believed strongly in his future, his probabilities of success were low. In truth, success was only really understood when Warner experienced it on the national stage.

How many times did he contemplate quitting, only to show back up the next day?

How many times did he feel he was letting down everyone who ever believed in him?

Now that Warner is enshrined in the Pro Football Hall of Fame, his sacrifices had to be worth it, right?

Do you have the same assurances?

No.

Despite the mounting evidence of failure, Warner found a way to break through his doubts and insecurities to face the challenges of the unknown and to keep fighting for what he wanted. He always found the push to keep going.

I can imagine Warner felt his circumstances sucked, worried that he sucked, or became frustrated that teams could not see his potential. Even worse, I can guarantee there were times he was frustrated he was not showcasing his tools.

Warner represents everything this book is about – the long journey to success and having to manage the expectations you place on yourself, the frustration you feel when you fall short of your potential, and the missed opportunities that keep piling up. That combination of frustration and continued disappointment is what I call "Suckville."

I am not sure what brought you to read this book, but I am confident it will change your life. The ups and downs of competition can get very lonely and unsettling. It can challenge every essence of who you are, especially if you allow it to define your identity. To be honest, I do not know many competitors who can keep it separate. When you cannot let go of your potential for what could be in your sport and life, you get stuck in the misery of missed opportunities and failed realities.

Your life is your competitive mindset. It is your greatest strength. I have never met someone who was truly mentally weak, not good at the mental side of performance, or could not find a way through doubt. Instead, you probably do not know how to focus on what you do great – or your mental weapons. If a coach gave you this book to help you see a different perspective on your game, better days are coming. You must continue pushing forward.

You will break free.

You will break free from the prison of your own mind, your personal Suckville, by changing the way you view your circumstances and opportunities.

I wish things were simple and you would achieve everything you desire. The unfortunate reality is things are so much more complicated than anyone could have imagined. Much more complex than anyone has honestly told you.

It does not matter where you want to succeed – in sports, business, or just life in general. There are many more moments of struggle, doubt, and worry than happiness, joy, and pride. That does not mean that success is so elusive that you cannot achieve it. Just that you better be mentally ready for the challenge.

Suckville is a state of mind, a belief that you are continually falling short of your magical potential and stuck in the frustration of endless disappointments. It is real, confusing, and painful. Suckville is a noun, a verb, and an adjective. It is a place of misery, a way to describe falling short, and a way of thinking. It is everything hard, all wrapped up in one location in the mind.

Suckville does not mean hopeless. There are levels of struggle that are truly unique to each person. You may have challenges staying positive, while a teammate may have difficulty focusing. The nature of the battle is genuinely personal. You may love the game with all your heart, and a colleague may find it hard to find joy in the game because of pressure to perform.

The state of mind representing Suckville may be long-lasting or episodic, hurt deeply, or be a simple hassle. What is essential to understand about the concept of Suckville is that it is your relationship with the game and how you feel about falling short of your actual ability or potential.

When you fail to reach the level of success you believe you are capable of, you get frustrated and disappointed. When that happens time and time again, the frustration becomes unbearable and unrelenting. It is an emotional sinkhole and describes the feeling of Suckville to perfection.

But you flirt with Suckville to ultimately have success. You cannot escape it. Nothing is ever easy. Throughout all your accomplishments, struggle and frustration have always been there.

Now, they simply seem to be more prevalent, more intense, and maybe even a bit more revealing about you.

Suckville.

Struggle.

Frustration.

Doubt.

Is it worth it? How much longer will it suck?

What I have learned through my pursuits and standing side-by-side with some of the world's best competitors is that the mere presence of doubts, frustration, and difficulty do not prevent you from achieving your goals. The fact you are aware of them tells me you are closer than you think. You must keep pushing forward, and I want to help you see things from a different perspective.

My journey defines Suckville. The years of working with elite competitors of every level, from every walk of life, and different countries worldwide have shown me what Suckville is all about. It is a state of mind that has significant impacts on the way you approach your desires.

You have probably been told your entire life that you are excellent at certain things. You have probably been able to find ways to win when needed. Circumstances have worked out for you.

Until now.

Something changed. Things have gotten harder, and you have become more frustrated with your performance. The joys of competition seem to be distant memories and the success that of a forgotten friend.

It is crucial to appreciate the influence of your expectations, self-belief, and confidence on your mindset. You probably think those three aspects constitute your mindset's essential components, but those factors are just contributors. Your mind is like a cast-iron skillet.

Chefs use cast-iron skillets because of their durability, ability to withstand intense heat and functional utility. You can cook eggs and then cook steak, and finish by baking cornbread. A cast-iron pan will last years if you take proper care of it.

Cast-iron absorbs the seasoning of each ingredient and seems to activate the depth of the flavors with each use. Years of experience highlight the complex flavors of the past into the next dish. Each period of intense heat reinvents the past into the present.

Your mindset is just like that.

Your mind is resilient, durable, and always a work-in-progress. With each use, it gets better. You can endure anything and, through every challenge, continually get better. In doing so, you learn to manage your expectations, build belief in your ability, and find ways to work through the struggle. Your mindset is more significant than what you expect. It creates success but does not expect it. It is about perspective and durability.

You were built for this challenge. I know it is hard right now, and it may get more demanding. But you will endure this struggle. You were created to do more and to achieve more extraordinary things.

Your expectations are causing most of your problems. For some reason, you believe things should be more accessible than they are, you should be having more success, and you should not need to work this hard. Those are the problem. Whether you think you should or should not, it is that hard.

I am the Suckville doctor. For years, I have specialized in helping competitors break out of their slumps, struggles, and frustrations to return to their desired level of play. No one seems to come to me when things are going great, only in times of struggle. I get it. When it is hard, you give me a call.

Maybe it is the fact that I am a clinician that helps me identify with my client's performance struggles. As a clinical psychologist, I explore both sides of the continuum – times of struggle and times of greatness. I do not just focus on performance; I focus on the person. How you think, behave, and work through the struggles is so important to me. You were not built for the easy days but the hard ones. I am going to help you tap into that magic in you.

Suckville is not a long-term destination. You will break through the struggles and frustrations. I will give you some helpful guidance in this book that I have based on my practical experience. It is not theory. Breaking free is about how you think, your overall perspective, and how to shift your mind toward opportunities and way from the struggles.

The Coin Flip

Before the kickoff of a football game, the head official brings the captains from each team to the middle of the field and conducts the coin flip. One team chooses "heads" or "tails." From there, the winning captain decides who gets the ball and which side of the field they want to defend. It is a relatively simple exercise, but it has significant implications for the rest of the game.

The team that wins the coin flip must choose to receive the opening kickoff and go on offense, to kickoff and go on defense, or defer the decision to the second half, which always means they will receive the second-half kickoff. Coaches are prepared for any coin flip outcome but have desired scenarios based on how they perceive their team's strengths line up against the opponent. Whatever happens, they adapt and start the game.

While the head coach may have wanted their defense on the field first because they have a tremendous defense, if they must start with the ball on offense, so be it. They adjust. If they lose the coin flip, it does not mean they are going to lose the game. Whatever happens, it is one small element in the game. It can have significant implications, but great teams adjust and move forward.

Your performance game has a coin flip right now. Things may have been hard, and you may have lost the love of the game or gotten more frustrated and impatient over your progress. Right now, you must choose to go on offense or defense, which side of the field you want to defend, and start the game. It is time for you to see that you have choices right now, and the new game is starting. It does not matter what has been going right or wrong. All that matters is that you get ready to play the game, learn from each experience, and fight to the end.

So, are you going to call "heads" or "tails"?

1

THE MAYOR OF SUCKVILLE

I heard this line from one of my clients. "I am the Mayor of Suckville," he said.

As an elite college athlete, my client was mired in such a brutal period of frustration and anger that he felt could not possibly get any worse. There was so much promise in his game, but his performance told a different story. No one ever warns you that it will be this hard until it is. And then you feel so alone.

He was in a slump of epic proportions and was so miserable that he worried he would never return to an acceptable level of play. Quitting the game was a serious option, even though he believed he would breakthrough at some point. The question was HOW?

He was referred by his collegiate coach to help find the spark that made him a brilliant recruit. Coach believed he was the missing piece for a national championship, but the player could not even beat one single player on the team. Both coach and player were frustrated and were begging for a breakthrough.

The player described his state of mind as cluttered, overwhelmed, and lost. The description was honest, heartfelt, and ridiculously accurate. There was little debate that his level of play did suck, and there were not many positive signs to suggest a brighter future was on the horizon. I asked him what he thought was wrong. He provided a complete laundry list of ailments, from specific mechanical errors to low confidence under pressure. The biggest issue was that he crumbled when trying to take his practice game out on the golf course during a tournament. His game would be flawless the day before the tournament and end up being a disaster as soon as it mattered.

His confidence was near rock bottom, but his self-image was even lower. He was embarrassed by the current state of his game and felt terrible his coach had placed so much faith in him.

"Do you think you suck?" I asked him.

"Suck? Doc, I am the Mayor of Suckville!" He replied.

I laughed out loud when he described himself as the "Mayor of Suckville," which made him laugh. That was the changing point of his career, right at that moment.

From that moment forward, he was willing to look at struggle differently. For far too long, he measured his overall performance by how close he got to his potential. The competition was not about the grind, winning or losing, or the simple joy of competing. Not for him. It was all a test to see if he could tap into that level of ability so many had promised he could achieve at some point. More hard work, more lessons, and more pressure led to a disaster formula.

Every day became a painful reminder that he was falling short. “Potential” became a dirty word in his vocabulary, and it eventually came to represent "failure."

It didn't matter that "potential" was some sort of mythical performance. Think about it – what is "potential?"

Who got to decide his “potential?”

Is there a “potential measurement system?”

If there is, please direct me because I have never seen one. Is “potential” defined compared to other competitors or just by yourself?

Coaches and parents seem to define “potential” all the time without even realizing it. They lovingly say things like "they have all the talent in the world, but just need to get their mind right," and "if they could just get rid of the silly mistakes, they could be successful." As if it were that easy.

For my player, he perceived the level of his "potential" around his technical proficiencies. His golf swing was beautiful and technically flawless. On the range. On the course was a different story. But on the driving range, his swing was often admired by teaching professionals as nearly perfect.

"If it is so good, then I must suck at using it when it matters, Doc. Why can't I figure out how to repeat it under pressure?" He lamented.

Every competition just served to remind him how far away he was from what he believed he could achieve. That is the problem with you too. More than likely, you are the Mayor of your own personal Suckville as well. You became the Mayor because something changed in your perspective.

The Accidental Shift

Your relationship with your competitive game is personal. No one can tell you what to feel, how to enjoy it, or what will improve your relationship with the game. That is the elegance of competition, however. It is up to you.

Competitors were born to compete. If you ask any former competitor what they miss after retirement, it is usually competition anxiety. It is never the moments of pure joy and success, but instead, the periods where their stomachs were tied in knots and their hearts were racing uncontrollably. You were born to compete.

Suckville is a state of mind that happens when the level of your performance no longer gives you satisfaction. Suckville is frustration, disappointment, and confusion all wrapped up into one painful emotion. And it all stems from the fear that you are falling short of your potential.

It has been my experience that the game progresses through different stages before getting stuck in Suckville. I will dive deeper into this later in the book, but it is necessary to understand that your negative mental shift did not happen because of one terrible performance. It built up through various outcomes that left you feeling frustrated because of the struggles in one aspect of your performance. Time and time again, those minor frustrations started to build the negative momentum of today.

Everything you do in the performance world starts with a desire to achieve something. Pursuing your goals can be exhilarating, and the sacrifices are worthwhile. However, over time, the pure innocence of your game becomes tainted by your expectations, the need to fulfill other's expectations, and the constant evaluations of proper play. When it starts to feel like a job, the struggle begins to settle in. With every struggle, the responsibility you feel to your team, coaches, family, and even yourself, intensifies. The consequences become more significant over time, and the struggles become amplified, and you feel the burden to compete.

I do not know why that happens to competitors, but it almost always happens. The competitive drive to solve the challenges of the game becomes more complex over time. Heightened expectations limit positive outcomes, and you struggle to find joy in the little things.

You have probably found yourself in this position quite often. Your competition becomes a job.

This mindset shift happens so quickly that you fail to realize it is happening. The grind starts to intensify. You may love the game and everything about it, but showing up to the gym or ballpark becomes a chore instead of an opportunity. The enjoyment drops, and expectations rise. Soon, it becomes an overwhelming burden.

I am not trying to paint the picture that competition is a brutal battle that will destroy your heart and soul. Giving everything for something you desire is one of the most rewarding things you can do. As a former competitor, I miss it terribly.

Every day, athletes, coaches, and business leaders call in to my office looking for help to break free from the burdens of their competitive life. What drives you to feel the struggle more than the joy is unique to you. Your performance could always be better, and when you get stuck, it is because it "should" be better.

Suckville lives and breeds in the world of "should." It thrives in the dark corners of your performance soul when you get frustrated that you did not perform as you have. Your struggles only amplify the pain of falling short of your perceived potential.

Minor difficulties in your game sound every alarm you have. If the game were fun, you would not be struggling like this, right? That is what everyone seems to say, that you should just have fun again. Despite all your efforts to see the game differently or do things better, the struggle seems to get rooted in your daily routines.

"Don't worry; you will eventually hit your potential" is code for "you keep falling short." When you become the Mayor of Suckville, the emotions of frustration and disappointment overrule desire and determination. There is so much you miss by focusing on your misery.

What separates the best from the rest is simple – they manage struggle better than everyone else. The most successful competitors experience significant challenges and fragile confidence like everyone else, but they use difficulty to optimize their processes. Their struggle does not forewarn danger, but instead, the best of the best uses their struggles to improve the details that drive their performance.

You must begin to see struggle differently. Do not anchor your dreams to the chains of "potential." Instead, see the opportunities as learning experiences across every competition.

The "should's" of performance do not lead to success, only frustration.

Imagine a competitive world and mindset where struggle, frustration, and disappointment no longer determine your future. It may seem far away, but that is only because of how you have started to see things.

Instead, I want you to think of a future where you –

- Know you are good enough to achieve what you desperately want,

- Can handle the stress and chaos of competition, and
- Find out who you are and learn to understand your unique way to face competition, a concept I refer to as your "psychological fingerprint."

You are not alone in your journey, and once you appreciate how you found yourself in Suckville, you will learn how to change your mindset. The simple positive mindset shift will help you succeed in ways you never thought were possible.

To Break Free from Suckville, I will help you get back to the basics of competition and start feeling the freedom of thought you had when you first started competing. You had an innocence then, and it is time to find it again.

You have come a long way, but I know you have more success in front of you. There is a long journey ahead of you, so use it to improve your performance standards. If you use every experience, you gain powerful wisdom on your mindset and process.

If you continuously see how far you must go, you will become burdened by the length of that journey. When you consistently focus on falling short of your potential, you will create so much physical and psychological tension that you will regress in high-pressure competitions. You will begin to fear failure and protect what you have with all your might. You will become paralyzed by what is in front of you and reject any success you have accomplished.

Becoming the Mayor of Suckville is not a badge of honor, nor is it the best place to be right now. It is time to build a better future by accepting that your reality no longer sucks. It is what it is.

Honestly, it's probably damn good! It is like the monster that is hiding in your closet. As a child, in the middle of the night, you were 100% certain there was a child-eating, flesh-devouring monster hiding in your closet, waiting for the right moment to attack. With every sound randomly resonating in the silence, you were sure it was going to get you.

But there was no monster. You realized that when you woke up in the morning and opened your closet door. Those intense fears were nothing more than a misinterpretation of something that posed no threat to you. Without knowing with certainty what the danger was, your mind went to the worst possible solution and created a magical story around the simplest of things.

The only way to Break Free from Suckville is to face it. Time to face the monster in your closet.

I am going to show you why you struggle and why your performance has been so miserable. You will understand why it is never personal and, more importantly, how to proceed with confidence and excitement through the clutter of your challenges. This book is not a "How To" book. I will share what I have learned from the best competitors and coaches globally and give you their insight into managing adversity.

Let go of the "Mayor of Suckville" title. It is time to become more than your biggest fears and doubts.

2

THE STRUGGLE YOU ARE IN

You are so close to doing great things, but it often feels like you are so far away from those moments. Progress gets clouded so quickly in frustration you forget your growth. You are so quick to judge yourself based on unrealistic expectations. That is the problem driving your struggles.

Tantalus, a prominent character of Greek mythology, exemplifies the nature of your struggle. Tantalus' psychological struggle can be a lesson for all humanity to appreciate the power of temptations of those blessings just out of reach.

Tantalus was the son of Zeus, who was the all-powerful king of the gods in Olympia. Tantalus was born wealthy, bestowed with all the abilities and potential in the world. As a mortal, Tantalus had opportunities that others did not; and over time, he lost perspective of his blessings, becoming impatient for more. The gods extended a rare dinner invitation to Tantalus because he was the son of Zeus. But Tantalus was not happy just dining with the gods. He wanted more.

Tantalus wanted to raise his social status among the other mortals, so he sought out the secrets behind the gods' powers, intentions, and actions. Having this priceless information, Tantalus could barter for more significant influence.

To capitalize, Tantalus hosted a dinner for the gods in the hopes he could find out their secrets and how he could use them for himself. Tantalus was not satisfied being a mortal. He wanted to be God-like.

He had an issue to consider, however. If the gods were all-knowing, there was a significant likelihood that they knew what he was up to, and they would stop and punish him. So, he devised a test to find out if they knew his intentions.

Tantalus devised a heinous plan – he would kill his son and serve him to the gods in the dinner stew. If the gods were genuinely all-knowing, they would realize the stew was tainted with the wrong meat.

In the end, the plan failed, and Tantalus got caught by the gods. Zeus punished Tantalus to a lifetime of misery for trying to deceive the gods.

The misery that Zeus prescribed was not just pain and suffering but rather an eternal life of temptation and anguish. Zeus punished Tantalus to live for eternity in Hades, the Greek equivalent of Hell, with an unquenchable thirst and hunger. This miserable punishment would be sufficient for most mortals but not for the transgressions of Tantalus. Zeus wanted more.

Not only was Tantalus going to be eternally thirsty and hungry, but constant temptations would surround him. He was forced to stand in a pool of water just below a succulent grape tree. When he would bend over to try to quench his thirst, the water in the pool would recede, and when he would stretch to grab one grape, the winds would blow the tree just out of reach of his hands.

He was constantly "so close and yet, so far away."

Zeus created the punishment to remind other mortals to be content with what they have and to resist the urge to become more than they were destined to be. Zeus did not want others to become so attracted to the successes of others that they would abandon their triumphs.

When you get tempted by the attraction for more, you often revert to the wrong means.

The Temptations Just Out of Reach

In your mind, there is a perfect level of your performance. You can see it. But that is all it is—a figment of your imagination.

There is no perfect performance. Competition never goes according to plan. The most successful competitors do not judge themselves by how easy things were but by how much they endured to succeed. You must let go of the "ideal" and focus on what you can make out of each day. Perfect performances are always just out of your reach.

The rewards of your sacrifices must be worth it, or you would never push through the doubts, frustrations, and misery of competition. What you are feeling right now will pass and open the doors to better performances and more enjoyable experiences. It is so hard to have perspective when you become immersed in the minute-by-minute struggle. The storms of frustration will let up, and the sun will shine soon. You must keep that perspective.

There are many times in your life when the path gets rugged and rocky. Do not let it deter you from your goal. Your struggle has an expiration date. The hardest thing about success is you do not know when you will achieve it. It is a mystery, while the struggle is a constant offender.

Every period of my life that I felt lost, overwhelmed, and confused eventually led to a breakthrough – usually more significant than I could ever anticipate. I guess I needed the struggle to appreciate the great moments in my life. I wish it would not have been hard, but I can look back and enjoy those moments more than ever.

As a high school athlete, it took me until my senior year to make the varsity team, and I only played for one season.

I did not get recruited to play college baseball. I was only offered a walk-on position at my local college.

I sat three years in college with minimal playing time and had to overcome an injury that challenged my ability with power, velocity, and command.

Academic advisors said I lacked the grades to be a good candidate for graduate school and look for lower-tier programs across the country. The problem was I had only one option that worked for my family. I had to go to the local university because my wife was in nursing school in town. Things were not promising at that time.

I needed someone to trust me. I really believed that if the opportunity was there, I would perform. Someone did, and while I was fortunate enough to be admitted to the local university, things only got worse. With a growing family, I struggled to complete my projects on time. I was slipping away, buried in pressure, and having debilitating panic attacks.

I knew what I wanted to do for the "rest of my life," but it was not happening fast enough for me.

There were many times that I was struggling.

However, the other side of struggle showed me to fight my fears to achieve something beyond my dreams. I never saw myself pitching in the College World Series, earning a Ph.D., or even running a consulting practice serving some of the best athletes and teams in the country. There were immense struggles along the way, many of which involved hard decisions to keep pushing or to walk away from the game.

Every battle made me better. Every challenge made me more determined.

You are in the heat of the moment right now. I do not want you to accept struggle or failure but to appreciate it instead. I want you to realize that you are not alone, and your frustrations are not uniquely miserable. Even the best struggle and get stuck in Suckville.

How Can Michael Phelps Be Depressed?

Michael Phelps is arguably the most dominant male athlete in modern sports. Across the five Olympic Games, he not only won but destroyed his competition in a variety of events, earning a total of 23 gold medals, three silver, and two bronze medals. Out of 28 total medals, 82% were gold! Phelps defeated rivals and world champions with such ease that he seemed to have it all together. His interviews were textbook displays of focus and intensity.

Yet, below the surface, he was hurting.

In 2016, Phelps documented his struggles in an edition of *ESPN: The Magazine* with writer Wayne Drehs (please check out the May 23, 2016 edition for more on this powerful story). The most decorated male Olympic athlete in history admitted he had suffered from depression for several years. Phelps stated that he often felt empty and isolated despite his fame and fortune as a worldwide and Olympic champion. The successes did not create happiness.

How can an athlete with everything, who has achieved more in their sport than anyone, be hurting so bad? The answer is not always known, much less understood. For most competitors, the drive to succeed begins with the right intentions, but over time, becomes clouded with expectations, pressures, and even alienation from the game. The amount of joy you have for the game will be the amount of pain you experience when things go wrong.

Success should get rid of struggle, right? I mean, if you have enough success, you should be able to get rid of all the hassles of life, the fear of failing, and the pain of criticism and judgment, right?

Many competitors believe that one successful outcome will break them out of their slump. As if one positive experience will make the future more prosperous or help you eventually find confidence.

It is a trap.

Would a gold medal in the Olympics make you happy? The consensus would be, "absolutely a medal would make me happy!" After so many years of sacrificing, there would have to be a validation to all that hard work.

Research and anecdotal evidence may suggest otherwise. Everything from news stories to documentaries captures the challenges of former Olympic athletes, even those with gold medals. Money does not buy happiness, and success does not protect you from the struggle.

In 1995, a group of researchers led by psychologist Thomas Gilvovich from Cornell University explored the immediate emotional responses to winning and losing. Gilvovich and his research team rated who they thought were happier based only on their appearance and body language during videotaped Olympic-medal ceremonies. Even though the students had no idea who earned a higher-ranking medal, the consensus was that athletes who won the bronze were generally happier with their outcome than those who won the silver medal.

The same researchers then did the study again for the Empire State Games, an Olympic-style competition for New York. The results showed that the athletes who had won a bronze medal appeared happier than those winning the silver. As you would expect, gold medal winners were rated the happiest, but why are the bronze medal winners perceived to be happier than silver medalists?

Expectations.

Falling short of potential.

"So close, but so far away."

David Matsumoto and his colleagues from San Francisco State University took the study a bit further. In the 2004 Olympic Games in Athens, Greece, the research team applied a computerized facial coding system to evaluate the judo competitors' psychological state immediately following their medal matches. Once again, silver medal winners seemed more disappointed than happy, while bronze medal winners were pleased.

How can a third-place winner be that happy? Happier than the second-place winner, the silver medalist?

Olympic athletes are no different than any other competitor on the planet. Ultimately, they want to win. But for Olympic athletes, winning is a tremendously low probability event that only happens once every four years. Winning a gold medal can be life-changing financially and in status circles (although, as stated above, that expectation often results in disappointment and depressed feelings).

Winning a silver means you lost to the winner. You are not the best in the world but the second-best. You are essentially the most successful loser.

But winning a bronze?

At least you are leaving with something. The athlete that comes in fourth was close enough to be on the podium but was not good enough to take home a prize, not the main prize, but ANY prize. The bronze medal winner compares their performance to the 4th, 5th, and 6th place finishers, and so on.

While they missed their ultimate goal, the struggle was worth it. Was it worth it for the silver medal winner? Being so close but not good enough can be a difficult mental challenge.

The sacrifices and struggles were present for both athletes to get them on the podium, but perspectives can be very different based on their perceived value of the outcome. Was it worth it for the silver medal even though they fell short of their ultimate victory?

It can be challenging for the silver medalist to be happy.

One more rep, one more hour of work may have made the difference. Very few people say they got beat after losing because it is easier to find something that caused you to lose instead of just admitting you were not good enough in that competition. But those critical conclusions make it harder to move on and be satisfied with the outcome.

The issue settles on a fact – what will make you happy?

At the beginning of the season, would the athletes be okay with winning a silver medal? Sure! But once in the heat of competition, perspective changes to what they did wrong, not what they did great. Performance happiness is always a moving target.

The journey of a competitor can be very challenging and exhausting. Whether you are an athlete, a coach, climbing the corporate ladder, or an entrepreneur, nothing prepares you for the desperation and doubt that accompanies desire. Competition gets more volatile the closer you get to your goal. At that point, you have more to lose. You can survive the desperate nights and painful mornings if you can keep hope for a prosperous future.

The Struggle is Real

Struggle is a part of life but critical for optimal performance. The mere presence of struggle does not forewarn a dangerous future or reflect the boundaries of your capabilities. It is nothing more than the clouds in the sky or the noise you hear in life. Be careful not to make it more than it is.

Internal and external difficulties become more prevalent and challenging as you have more success in the game. You must realize that struggle must be present to have success. You cannot escape it.

Things will not always go your way. Your perspective in the present struggle determines your response. By getting your mind focused on the moment, the struggle becomes a catalyst for success.

What does it take to make that happen? It sounds simple – you must see yourself as the ultimate creator of your future. It does not matter what is happening around you; it is what is happening INSIDE you that matters.

With each step forward, there will also be steps backward. Do not conclude that the steps backward are roadblocks to your success. Instead, realize that with each step forward, you are getting closer to the goal.

You will get frustrated and discouraged at times. Just because you lose positive momentum in the moment does not mean that you will fall short of your future goals. There will up and downs, so do not get caught up in the negative emotions.

Keep pushing forward. You cannot stop. It may not become what you think it will, but when has it ever really arrived as you anticipated it.

Instead, allow your success to be whatever it needs to be. It is what it is - nothing more and nothing less.

What are you carrying with you on your journey – burdens or tools? Every experience leaves you the opportunity to see success and failures as either struggles or catalysts. Burdens or tools?

Accept the struggle. Understand the challenges. Appreciate the difficulty of the journey. Do not stop until it becomes something you want.

Turn Chicken Sh&t Into Chicken Salad

How many things can you endure before giving up on your dream?

Stacy Brown did not give up, and if you love chicken salad, you will be thankful she never gave in to the dangers of entrepreneurship. Brown is the founder of the fast-casual restaurant, Chicken Salad Chick. Starting in the college town of Auburn, Alabama, Brown's story would be more relatable if she was an Olympian than a restauranteur, but it is remarkable.

I first learned of Brown's story on the entrepreneur-centered podcast *How I Built This by Guy Raz*. Raz explores the valuable lessons of successful entrepreneurs as they built their businesses. Most highlight the remarkable grit, determination, and desire of building a business from scratch, and Raz probes for those moments when they wanted to quit and walk away from their dreams. Each story has those moments when doubt threatened their future.

Brown's story was not any different from other entrepreneurs, but it may have been a little bit more impressive. When many others may have found the challenges to be too difficult, she continued to find a way.

During the interview, Brown articulated her plight as a divorced mother of four looking to earn extra money. Because she needed to be home for her children, she needed to create an income stream from her house. She decided to start making chicken salad and sell it door-to-door in her neighborhood. What started as a strategy to earn extra money became a demanding venture. Satisfied customers became community champions, and her brand exploded.

As her chicken salad caught more people's attention, so did her problems. After several months of around-the-clock production in her home kitchen, the Alabama Health Board shut down her home-based business.

Evidently, it is illegal to sell food made in an at-home kitchen in the state of Alabama. Who knew?

While Brown was disappointed, she was not defeated. She was motivated to find a solution.

Brown found a small building with a full commercial kitchen available in a rundown part of town. While it was not in the best neighborhood in the city, she did not need a prime location. All she wanted was a chance to make her popular chicken salad as her customers were knocking on her door to place orders. Her business was no longer a side hustle.

Brown needed to formalize all of her business affairs before she got overwhelmed by the legitimate organizational financial operations. She was fortunate to find an accountant who had experience with small businesses and had the time and interest to help her. What she did not know was that she had hired her future husband. The late-night work sessions fostered a personal relationship that transformed her business and prepared her vision to expand into new markets. Chicken Salad Chick was hatched.

In her new building and with a new business partner (and husband), Chicken Salad Chick took over the Auburn, Alabama community. They worked around the clock and managed orders, led employees, and raised a family, but the rapid growth of the business was taking a toll.

The Browns partnered with a national franchising organization to expand their business into out-of-state markets. Despite all the wonderful marketing promises from the national company, the Browns were disappointed and frustrated. The national organization failed to generate any new business and left the Brown's needing to break the contract and take control of their company. The problem was that to break the contract required the Brown's to buyout the remaining time left in the agreement. They did not have the money to gain their business freedom.

The Browns sought financial support from every person they knew. They knew it was going to be a miracle, as they had to secure the buy-out funding by the deadline in the contract or lose the business. The scenario was dire for the Browns.

In the proverbial 24th hour, the Browns received a phone call from an older gentleman who had heard their story and had declined to support their request just a few days ago. But he could not forget them or stop thinking about their story. He was now willing to invest.

Chicken Salad Chick was saved and flourished. The Browns, bolstered by their new financial support, rapidly grew the restaurant through regional franchises across the southeast. The stores served the famous chicken salad and a variety of new flavors, providing a full-service restaurant with chic feel.

Who would have thought that chicken salad would be so popular?

The story does not end there. As the Browns were growing their business, their lives took a massive hit. While planning a large benefit concert for cancer research, Kevin Brown was diagnosed and quickly passed away from colon cancer. Stacy's emotionally supportive co-leader was gone.

The Browns could not seem to break away from struggle. A dream that rose out of financial struggle and became a regional powerhouse, once again fell back into uncertainty and drama. Running a business is difficult but growing with the amount of challenges the Browns experienced only made it more improbable to succeed.

Stacy Brown continued to persevere and push forward with Chicken Salad Chick. In the fall of 2019, Brown and her investment team sold Chicken Salad Chick to private equity. The company continues to thrive as it executes national franchising opportunities.

Stacy Brown's mindset gave her the power to push forward despite her circumstances and challenges. She did not have an easy road but never backed down. Even when she thought she had no options, she kept pushing forward. Each challenge became an opportunity to empower herself and find a way towards new solutions. You could say Brown took "chicken sh&t and turned it into chicken salad."

How Much More Do You Have?

How much more do you have to give when the competition continues to beat you down?

If you have not had that thought, you are not pushing hard enough.

When your mind gets worn down, you get flooded with negative thoughts. They challenge your progress, make you doubt if you are good enough, and how you compare to others.

- *Great competitors do not doubt as I do.*
- *Great competitors do not have problems with their families.*
- *The greats do not suffer with relationships because they feel conflicted.*
- *Great competitors do not suffer from their self-esteem and identity.*
- *Great competitors do not suffer from depression and anxiety.*
- *Great competitors never lose the love of the game. They live for 5 am workouts and love their sport.*

But…

The truth is different.

- *Great competitors struggle.*
- *Great competitors suffer.*
- *Great competitors often feel lost in relationships.*
- *Great competitors have their hearts broken.*
- *Great competitors have crushing doubts.*
- *Great competitors are scared to death of letting people down.*

Every competitor I have worked with struggles with the same conflicts.

- *Am I good enough to compete?*
- *Can I handle the stress around me and manage the fears, doubts, and insecurity inside my head?*
- *Can I manage future challenges and persevere?*

The struggle associated with success is never personal. It is not the exception either. The battle is developmental at the core.

Your struggle is unique to you, but you are not alone. The fact that you are reading this book suggests that you want to learn more about getting better despite the struggles you have experienced. You are stuck in Suckville, but I will guide you out of it. You are not alone in your journey, and once you appreciate how you found yourself in Suckville, you will learn how to change your mindset to succeed in ways you never thought were possible.

3

MANAGING UNCERTAINTY

McDonald's, the world's leading fast-food restaurant, has maximized sales and consumer interest by leveraging seasonal product offerings. McDonald's converted a failed menu item, a barbecue processed-pork sandwich, into a cult favorite through clever marketing campaigns, but only during certain times of the year. The simple fact that you could not get the sandwich when you wanted it raised the demand for the McRib.

Initially introduced in 1981, the consumer response to the McRib was rather tepid. Folklore suggests that McDonald's created the McRib to counter a national chicken shortage, delaying the release of their highly anticipated fried chicken product, the McNugget. But the McRib never gained positive market share, and by 1985, it was off the menu.

In 1994, McDonald's marketing department decided to reintroduce the McRib as a limited-run item only across the country. There was a wrinkle, however. They only planned to release the McRib at random times and in different regions of the country. Now that the McRib was special and limited, sales increased significantly. All of sudden, customers had to get a McRib because they had no idea when they would have the chance again.

The result was powerful and sustaining. The limited-release McRib outperformed any period when it was the standard menu. Because the customers wanted it, they limited its production. Genius!

Why would a randomly released product be so successful when it failed as a regular menu item?

Novelty.

Uncertainty.

Inconsistency.

It is a psychologically based strategy that I have seen work in a variety of different settings. Companies need to create a plan that drives interest and limited availability creates demand. When products are always available, they get dull because of the surplus and access.

Psychologists have conceptualized this as "schedules of reinforcement." Derived from the teachings of behavioral psychologist, B.F. Skinner, how a subject (a person, research participant, etc.) gets rewarded or punished will determine the probability of the desired behavior to continue or stop.

If you want a behavior to continue, reward that behavior. If you want the behavior to stop, punish it. Those are simple.

If you want to avoid an undesirable event, like having to do extra chores or stay late at work and doing something positive or constructive allows you to avoid the unpleasant, that would be called negative reinforcement. In a sense, doing the desired behavior will increase because you are able to avoid something unpleasant. For instance, if you clean your room (desired behavior), you do not have to do the dishes. But if you do not clean your room on time, you will have to do the dishes after dinner instead of going to play, and no one wants to do dishes instead of playing with friends. Psychologists refer to this level of learning as Operant Conditioning.

Both positive and negative reinforcement maintain positive behaviors. But rewards start to lose their luster over time. If you can get the same reward or benefit without doing the correct behaviors, you will start cutting corners. Doing the hard things to get the desired reward can be challenging, so looking for an easier path is expected. The fire in your belly slowly loses its intensity because you can have some success without the sacrifices. Psychologists call this "motivational drift."

Motivational drift begins because the sacrifices for success are too significant. It is hard to continue giving your full effort day after day, but it is even harder when the results are inconsistent and unpredictable. When it takes longer to see the positive results, it is hard to stay motivated.

When you get frustrated because results are slow to show up, it is very difficult to stay committed to the plan. It is a cycle that normally begins because the results are unpredictable and not fast enough. Eventually, your impatience will short-circuit your motivation and effort, and you will start to look for short-cuts to the process. But it does not work, and you struggle more.

Few players ever connect the dots that they are not having success because they are cutting corners. It is easier to blame something or someone, focus on the unfair factors out of your control, or how hard the game is. You will start obsessing about the uncertainty of competition.

The Only Certainty Is Uncertainty

All success is uncertain and rarely follows a consistent or predictable schedule. The only sure thing is that it is uncertain.

To this date, your rewards and struggles have not been consistent or fair. Some days produce one positive result, and the next day it produces a failure. Believe it or not, that inconsistency is what drives you to want it more!

If rewards are inconsistent, then the impact will become more powerful. If your rewards, such as feeling confident, winning games, or earning a starting role, are possible, you will keep fighting for them. Just because there is a chance, the effort is worth it. The reason is apparent – if there is the hope of a positive outcome and it is worth fighting for, you will continue pushing forward through the uncertainty.

Success is what psychologists call a variable schedule of reinforcement, which is the most potent reinforcement model for driving behavior. Some days, the game goes your way, and it feels great. Other days, you feel lost, and you are miserable. But the slightest chance it will feel good again brings you to the competition with hope and dreams.

It is like playing the slot machines in Las Vegas. The slots are inconsistent enough to make you sit there for days hoping you will win with your next pull of the handle. Casinos are experts at using every psychological trick to make you believe that you will win soon! The sounds of bells, flashing lights, and the attraction of large winning pots only make you believe you are the reason you will win because it is your time. Despite the potential of having to pay a large payout, the casino wants you to believe that you could be next, so get to playing!!!!

Uncertainty is addictive in some environments and maddening in others. The simple act of not knowing is what drives most competitors crazy.

McDonald's successfully leveraged this approach with the McRib. You better get the McRib when it is released, or you will have to wait a long time to get it again.

Urgency!

Just like:

- Girl Scout Cookies
- The novelty of the Christmas/Hannukah season
- Streaming options on Netflix and Amazon Prime that get taken away after a while
- Opening days in sports
- The Pumpkin Spice Latte at Starbucks
- And other seasonal offerings.

Success and struggle are based on variable reinforcement schedules as well. You will never control everything to succeed, and you can never prevent every aspect of failure. Sometimes you play great and win; other times, you struggle. It often defies logic. Yet, you continue to show up, sometimes at the expense of your self-esteem.

The inconsistency of success drives the perception of struggle. It magnifies the misery of an off-day, a slump, and a painful stretch of competition because you cannot fully grasp the uncertainty of success. One day, you felt a certain way, warmed up with a new routine, and that led to victory. But the next day, you repeated everything verbatim and failed. What you ate did not matter today, even though it seemed to matter yesterday.

Success and failure are not under your complete control. They are products of probability, not absolute certainty. One thing is certain – it is more challenging than you ever thought.

Your expectations are crushing your progress.

Just because you have the skills and talent to succeed does not mean that you will. Far too many are married to their skills, expertise, and overall abilities and think that those alone will result in success. But that is the trap.

Yes, skills and talents matter, but what matters more is how you use those skills and talents to face the uncertainty of competition. When you are so stuck on proving your abilities and talents, it is like doing a beauty contest. It becomes more about the image and not the application.

The most successful competitors manage struggle better than you. It is as simple as that. The greats have used their struggles to launch consistent success. The struggle did not evade them. They did not have it easier than you either. They just took care of their business while going through their challenges.

You are trapped because you are too worried about the presence of struggle and not paying attention to the purpose behind it. You are terrified that it means you are not good enough. The fight is the norm and not perfection. Your enemy is self-doubt.

This realization should not scare you, depress you, or crush your outlook—quite the opposite. If you know the enemy, you can build a plan to destroy it.

The most significant struggles in your life have created the person you are today. That truth does not make the misery and frustrations you feel when you are continually falling short more comfortable to swallow, but it is true.

If you know the struggle will happen, why does it surprise you when it happens? Shouldn't you be prepared for the struggle as much as you dream about success?

The struggle never lives in isolation. The psychological aspects involve increased doubts, frustration, confusion, and anger. It also has reduced faith in the future, belief in self, and trust in the process. It is dirty, cluttered, and exhausting.

Struggle ultimately changes your perspective on reality. It distorts your view of your progress and the competitive world all around you.

When you struggle, you get stuck in the misery of competition and become frustrated that progress is not going faster. I am sure that you thought it would be different for you because you have done the work, put in the hours, and not cheated the process. With every success, you simply fell for the flirtation of more success. The struggles cannot last forever.

Eventually, it would all go your way.

But it hasn't.

I know first-hand the feeling of struggle. I was never good enough to play at the level that I did. I needed good breaks to get into graduate school and needed some great connections to land the country's top psychology internship/residency. Despite the success, I was always worried I was falling short.

If I had only worked harder…

If I had only eaten right…

If I had only written more…

If I had only exercised more…

If I had only…

I rarely left a game with the feeling that I crushed it. I always felt that I had survived, but I still wanted more. My angst drove me to do more but also wore me down.

My goal is to provide you a platform that can get to the core of your performance issues but do it in a way that will relate to your journey. Deep down, you are coming up short time and time again.

When you struggle to become what you believe you should be, you are fighting an internal battle. You are fighting for what you love in the broader sense, but the game is not loving you back. You are putting on a face of perseverance and courage but struggling with the battle, wearing down your pride, energy, and endurance.

The internal struggle is more significant than the competitive environment. It is personal.

Over the years, I have gained additional insight into helping clients break free from their self-limiting beliefs and resist growth patterns. The reason is apparent – I have been there personally.

I know the zip code of Suckville like it was the first house where I raised my children. I know it, and I know how it grabs hold of you.

It will take a shift in your mindset, which may be the most formidable challenge you have faced. It is easy to do something different but challenging to think differently. The patterns of frustration are the reasons you in this situation. You must learn to give up the known consistencies in your life.

4

WHAT IS SUCKVILLE?

Tell me if you have heard this before, "It is all mental at this point. You have everything you need to succeed, but you prevent yourself from the success you deserve. Eventually, you will just trust the tools you have."

I can guarantee that you have had a coach or friend tell you something like this. The game is supposed to be fun, but I have not seen many enjoy it when immersed in the minutiae of performance. It is dirty, miserable, and at times, downright terrifying.

"It is all mental" when you struggle but never "all mental" when you succeed, is it?

I despise that line of thinking. It is always mental. Everything you do, good or bad, is a combination of physical and mental processes. The problem thinking that the mental side is the reason you are struggling is that it changes how you see things. When you believe something is missing, you only see evidence of that in everything you do. All you start to see is a struggle.

The journey out of Suckville is going to be complicated. It always is. It has never been easy.

Never been easy in your past and never will be in your future. But there is a way out.

The Mental Trap

I sat down with a prominent professional athlete when he took an extended leave from the game. Things had gotten so hard for him that he had fired members of his training team for a spark and fresh energy. Those changes did not work, and he hired me as a last-ditch effort. When he first made it to "the league," the game was so new and fun. Unfortunately, over time, that changed. What prompted the time with me was that he was considering retirement.

As a generational player with a significant contract, quitting would leave a considerable amount of money on the table. The problem was not the money, though. He was miserable. He loved the game in theory, but he hated the game. Every part of training and competition had become a burden.

He always prided himself on being the first person in the gym through high school and college. He watched game film, put in extra work, and watched videos of the greats, trying to decipher the lessons of the best-of-the-best. The outside distractions were there, but he was not afraid of the late nights because he would counter it with early mornings. Every game provided a new opportunity to go against a player who he had grown up watching.

Challenges in the game were just that – challenges. But over time, they became hassles, burdens, and difficulties. Things got stale. He dreaded going to the gym, the facility, and each competition led to a pit in his stomach of dread. His body language projected intense stress, built from managing the pains of pressure to live up to his past and the expectations of a successful future. While the pressure seemed to come from the media, his agent, and the franchise, he put so much pressure on himself that everything else was just background noise.

As he struggled, he started looking at every aspect of his performance. All he could see were disappointments and shortcomings. Nothing was fun, and no one was supportive. The 5-10% of performances that were challenging consumed 95% of his attention. It was all he could see.

What changed?

He still embodied world-class athletic ability and game-changing talents.

"Just go out and have fun again," everyone said.

How do you do that?

It is not that easy.

Sure, the game was getting harder. As a professional athlete, he was getting older, and there were more distractions outside the game. His career path was no longer exhilarating and stimulating. It had become a job, a burden, and a responsibility. His improvements in the physical side of the game could not outperform the hole he was digging in the mental game.

For him to break free of the burden, he needed a change in perspective. I could not magically make him enjoy the game again, but I could get him to see his challenges differently. Those challenges were not what he thought – they were not more challenging for him, unique to him, or unfair. Each challenge and difficulty were his personal experience with the game. They were always there, but now, he was more aware and frustrated with them. They seemed to have more significant consequences now, and the pain was more intense.

By shifting his focus, he changed the lens through which he viewed his life.

The struggles were the same, but the impact changed. They were no longer personal and limiting. I helped my professional athlete see that he could be mentally or psychologically flexible, adapting and adjusting to the ever-changing demands in his life.

I wanted to shift his power back into his hands.

His internal dialogue was no longer "Why does this keep happening to me?" and it shifted to "What can I do with what I am facing today?" For him, it gave him a purpose each day.

It takes a mental switch to see the challenges in your life differently. You own that switch, and it takes no talent to use it. Having more success does not make things easier, and neither does tearing everything apart and starting over. It takes you continuing to push forward and simply changing your mental approach.

The Mental Grinder

Millions of thoughts bombard your consciousness throughout the day, with 99% never hitting your awareness or focus. The fact that you can direct your attention where you want, away from attention-grabbing distractions, is what makes human beings unique from other species. It is that level of mental control that makes humans unique. Psychologists refer to this as "executive functioning," which is the cognitive ability to have higher-level thinking, organization, and attentional control. The easiest way to look at it is this way – your mind goes where your attention flows.

Shifting your thinking may seem daunting. It may feel impossible with everything hitting you at once and the pressures making you feel like you are drowning in the sea of performance. But it is possible. Shifting your mindset is a skill you develop over time, through periods of great ease and other times of challenge. Each moment, you have the choice of creating your perspective, directing your focus, and giving total effort.

Your mind is like a meat grinder. It blends memories to form your past experiences into a story you tell yourself, becoming your identity and self-image. Every experience becomes a building block for your future and not the sledgehammer you have been using. It is time to see it differently.

It takes significant work to shift your thinking.

Being highly judgmental, emotional, and reactive is often the default. It is easier to take things personally than to face challenges with purpose and perspective.

Success will not make you happier, make it easier, or get rid of the pain. It is merely a trap unless you shift your thinking. Stop thinking that one great game or one outstanding performance will break you free.

The individual successes you experience will not magically change you. The result is not the key. The process you worked through to succeed at the end is what matters.

Unfortunately, your performance perspective is what gets eroded. You forget the little moments that produce your results. They start to blur together, discounting the monumental choices that seemed inconsequential now but led you to push through the chaos.

There is reality, and there is emotion. Emotion shifts your perspective of reality, seeing only what you emotionally feel. When you are deep in the struggle like my professional athlete discussed earlier, your mindset becomes focused on difficulty and concern, carrying the burden of continued struggle. As a result, you become emotionally raw and biased towards difficulty.

Those negative emotions that you start to feel only break you down further. They continually remind you that you are falling further and further away from the standards you believe you should achieve. You see what others are doing, and you get reminded you are falling short. The newness wears off over time during the journey, and the motivation that got you started on this journey is never the motivation that keeps you pushing forward.

The motivation that got you started was the desire to achieve something, but once you get the short-term success and the pain of uncertainty is gone, your motivation fades. If you are not careful, you will find yourself back in the sludge of struggle in no time. That is why the journey is so arduous and exposes every aspect of who you are. All it is doing is highlighting your insecurities, doubts, and struggles.

Why is that?

Why is it that we allow those negative emotions to come in without any resistance?

You do not have to be perfect to be successful. It is not all or nothing, black or white. Even the most minor victories can help you be successful. But you must start looking at the small wins to start breaking out of

Suckville. Your focus and perspective matter.

Focus instead on what you will do because there will always be more. There will always be a struggle, and there will always be challenges. Change your mindset from "why is this happening?" to "what do I need to do while it is happening?"

When you get caught in the "why" of competition, you lose focus and motivation, just when you need them the most.

The burden of the journey kills the motivation of most people. It takes them out of the challenge.

Why are you on this journey?

What do you have to do to achieve it?

It is not supposed to be easy. It is supposed to be a journey. You must remind yourself of the motivation that got you started. And use that motivation daily.

Do not allow your mind to believe that secondary motivations will push you out of this. The secondary motivations are those little successes that make you feel better but do not get you anywhere substantial. Focus on the step you are going to take next, not the one that you just took. See the challenge right in front of you, not the ones past or those in your future.

Competitors spend so much time on the factors that do not give the most significant returns. Far too often, they get distracted when they feel a little bit of relief instead of staying the course for the real goal. You need to evaluate if what you are doing now produces the results you want or wastes too much energy on things that do not matter.

You must give yourself more compassion along the way. Over time, as you experience more struggles, you need to provide yourself with more understanding to maintain your motivation. You need to act like your own teammate and give yourself some support.

When you look at your current journey, where you are, and the goals you want to achieve, it is easy to compare your progress to those of others. But be careful. Your memory nor your comparison lens are as good as you think they are.

It was not as easy as you remember it. And it sure as heck was not as easy for everyone else.

When you romanticize what others are doing, you must be willing to take on their burdens too. When you look back at their past journeys, are you ready to take on all the hardships that they overcame to achieve where they are?

Do not just see the rejoicing. See the effort that went into it.

You must live fully immersed in your current journey and only use the past as a reminder of what you can accomplish. If you hang on to the past and obsess about the greatness of others, you will keep beating yourself down. Focus on the steps in front of you and the process you are building through the journey.

The results are not always in your conscious control, but the process you refine along the way will serve you for a lifetime. Keep learning to do things better. Just stay focused because sometimes you make mistakes simply by trying to be better.

The Fizzle of New Coke

The Coca-Cola Company is a worldwide soft drink brand. With a wide variety of flavor profiles, Coca-Cola has a universal appeal that has stood the test of time. Since the late 1880s, the beverage brand has dominated the market share and served as a cultural foundation for generational causes. In parts of the country, if you say you want a "Coke," people will ask you what kind of brand name has become interchangeable for any carbonated soft drink.

The power of the Coca-Cola Company is their understanding of their markets and manipulating consumer behavior. With effective advertisements planted across television and print media to product placements in movies, there is no doubt the power of the red can with the white wave. Coca-Cola has spanned generations in America and united the world with commercials featuring the jingle "if you could buy the world a Coke."

Despite solid customer loyalty, the company made a massive strategic mistake in the summer of 1985, after seeing its market share and consumer preference erode in favor of its bitter rival, Pepsi. PepsiCo, the parent company of the soda Pepsi, launched a marketing campaign featuring blind taste tests showing nearly three-quarters of tasters preferred Pepsi over Coke. Coke loyalists were on television admitting they liked the flavor of Pepsi better.

As a result, market share shifted towards Pepsi, and a whole new generation of soda drinkers became Pepsi loyalists. Coca-Cola was losing generations of buyers, and the future looked bleak.

Coca-Cola Company felt they needed a strategic shift to regain their lost market share. The company feared that consumers no longer preferred the original recipe of Coke and reacted by significantly changing the formula. The alteration to the formula was the first significant change to the historical formula, done solely to resist the success of their main competitor. It was a disaster and ultimately became viewed as one of the greatest marketing blunders in United States history.

While taste tasters had been picking Pepsi in blind taste tests, Coca-Cola overlooked their brand loyalty, a significant factor in purchasing behavior. Coke had tremendous brand loyalty that extended beyond the soda flavor, and the company failed to understand that.

Coke customers were unhappy in large numbers. The publicity of the new formula was primarily negative, and customers felt abandoned as if they had lost their trusted safety blanket. Coke loyalists did not want to purchase Pepsi and were upset by the changes.

The Coca-Cola Company had to respond to its customers' criticism and bring back the old Coke formula. They repackaged it as Coca-Cola Classic, and I can remember where I was when I heard the news. I was one of the unhappy customers who was thrilled with the return of the original formula!

It was financially expensive, but it was more costly with consumer confidence. For years, Coke loyalists were not happy with the decision to change their beloved product. Why would they change so drastically?

Coca-Cola reacted to the competition by abandoning what it did well. While their concern was losing valuable market share, the company failed to appreciate the real reasons why a customer purchased Coke. Imagine if they had just decided to better understand their customers instead of changing the iconic formula!

For the Coke loyalists, it was more than a soft drink. It was a lifestyle.

One of the most incredible things we have is our uniqueness, those small variabilities from the norm and the standard. Each of us must identify and embrace our variability while going through Suckville. You have your way, your strengths, and your own experiences. It is not for someone else to say how you need to do things. Live your journey, not theirs.

It is more important than ever to identify the uniqueness that you have. Your variances create your "normal." That is when you can determine your greatness.

When you try to become what everyone wants you to be, you lose your creativity and unique superpowers.

Conformity is not about being average. The opinions of others define the concept of conformity, not your vision. If you do things the way you have always done them, you will spend significantly more energy trying to change that behavior. If you conform to how everyone else performs, it will be even harder to change and break away from the pack.

I have found that the process of emerging from Suckville always works better when you fully embrace who you are. When struggling, the mind gets overwhelmed with possibilities and becomes attracted to feelings of relief, so much so that it fails to find its capabilities to succeed.

You lose yourself when you lose the sense of time and allow your impatience to take over. You want it faster and easier instead of waiting for success to emerge. You must avoid the constant timeline analysis and let go of the frustration that it is not happening fast enough. It is going to be hard, and it is going to take longer than you think.

The Climb

Jamie Clarke is a modern-day explorer and high-performance adventurer. He has conquered the world's Seven Summits, climbed Mount Everest on two occasions, and survived the Empty Quarter on camelback. As part of the Arabian Peninsula, The Empty Quarter is not for the faint of heart, as it took 40 days for Clarke and his small team of explorers to cross the largest desert in the world. Clarke's perspectives have motivated entrepreneurs, inspired the 2018 Stanley Cup Champion Washington Capitals, and made him an in-demand keynote speaker.

I had Clarke on my podcast to talk about the psychology of facing immense challenges. Understanding that fear is the most potent motivator for pushing on, Clark stated that the fear of quitting kept him moving forward. He could never allow himself to look back and accept that he stopped before it was necessary. Knowing when to quit is essential, as he turned around one hundred meters from the peak of Mount Everest because the risk of proceeding was too high.

According to Clarke, acknowledging the struggle is the first and most crucial step. Too many do not appreciate the difficulty of the challenge and assume the struggle reflects their inadequacies. You must choose to continue, stop, or find support to keep pushing.

Clarke is not implying that quitting is for the mentally weak because there are times that quitting is the most prudent decision you can make. Once you choose to endure the misery and keep pushing forward amidst the challenges, you must determine the next step. You reframe and refocus in the heat of the moment.

Reframing the situation and finding the purpose in the moments of misery allowed him to persevere through the most significant challenges in the world. Simply put, it is hard to keep going without immediate results. You must learn to reframe the situation and keep pushing. It is never easy, nor will it ever be dull. Success is hard, and it gets more complicated with more experience.

What Exactly Is Suckville?

Suckville is a state of mind that changes your reality for your past and your perception of the future. It is not a sign of being mentally weak or lacking the ability to succeed in the future.

Suckville is how you view your progress and the understanding of your skill sets. Suckville is temporary, even though it feels painfully forever. Being frustrated with your progress does not mean you will not succeed, but you must understand the nature of your angst with your game.

Suckville started because you wanted more, stopped doing the little things that drove success, and changed the way you looked at your progress. Instead of seeing growth, you recognized evidence that you are falling short of your ability and potential. As a result, you believed you needed success to build your confidence to compete for your best.

You may think that success and experience will make things easier, but reality says that the more you progress forward, the more challenges you will find. New opportunities will arise, and new challenges will materialize, continuing to challenge the core of who you are every day.

It boils down to your mindset and changing your perspective to break free.

I received a call from a prominent agent in the golf industry a few years ago for a player who was really struggling. This former "can't miss" player, "Jack," was struggling to make cuts. He was so frustrated that he had changed coaches several times and desperately sought salvation from anyone willing to help.

When I get a call like that, it always takes me back to my struggles when I was competing. I can feel the intensity of the pain and remember the desperation as if it were happening to me right now.

At the beginning of new consulting relationships, I must separate the hysterics and fear from reality. I understand their pain, but it is never as bad as they think it is. I have found time and time again that fear and frustration are much greater than the reality of any performance. Emotions magnify every error and minimize every success when stuck in Suckville.

For Jack, the issue was not his play in the moment. He was not playing terribly, but when he struggled, his mind immediately shifted to the anger. There were unrealistic expectations that he had to live up to in order to please his team, family, media, and sponsors. Before achieving any actual results, there were so many companies and coaches investing in his promising future based on his "potential." No one was advising him on the present moment. A lousy shot was not just a bad shot but a sign that he was letting everyone down. Jack was failing, and it was all on him.

Misery and Suckville became his identity. Jack was typically "happy go lucky," but he had soured on the game and tour over the past year. He showed up at the last minute to practice and found every reason to skip practice sessions. His attitude sucked. He was miserable and a black cloud hung around him constantly.

Jack lost it one day when his mother called, worried about his mental state. She was concerned because he looked terrible on television, was never smiling, and looked worn down. He was not having fun, and it showed.

On good days, he attributed his success to being "lucky," and any negative performance was because he "had lost his talent." He broke down when she called. He just wanted to play the game again and break free from the game that was breaking him down. You never know the whole story when you see someone else competing. Competition is brutal for everyone. Each competitor goes through their own "something" and battle times when they lose their power over the game.

I needed to get Jack back to his training plan, to play for him, and build his resilience to struggles. My primary recommendation was to eliminate the number of people in his professional and personal relationship circle, limiting the access of sponsors, outsiders, media, and consultants that significantly cluttered his mind. I wanted to reintroduce him to the game he loved as a kid. He had to take control.

It worked.

Not as fast as he wanted at the outset, but right on plan. He was emotionally stable and started building relationships outside the game. His family instituted a "no golf talk" policy, and it provided him a haven to be a human, not a professional golfer.

What an incredible connection. I wanted him to find the joy of the game again, and he did. How he got there and what he associated it to did not matter to me. The fact was he began to see the game differently.

I guarantee your story is not much different. I do not know why you are stuck in Suckville, but there is a lesson in there for you.

Why Do You Have Pain in Your Life?

The emotional experiences and the struggles have values associated with them. They hurt for a reason. But focusing on the hurt robs the understanding behind the pain. Stop running from the discomfort and start learning from it.

Your performance life is not near completion. You have not entirely written your story. There is a lot more to accomplish.

Do not assume that you are anywhere near the end of your story. The pain you are in right now may be miserable, but you have more to accomplish.

You are struggling because of the unsuccessful, repetitive patterns you must break. You must be patient for the new processes to work. Stop looking for quick fixes and start focusing on long-term sustainability.

Struggle is a reminder to find the strengths within you. You have all the tools you need to succeed, but you have not learned how to access them yet. The answer does not have to be complicated.

Throughout the subsequent chapters, I will take you on a deep dive into

Suckville to understand how it developed, its symptoms, and how to break free. I have helped many players break free of their Suckville, and I am confident if you work on your mindset, do the little things that build success, and embrace where you are, you will break free too.

5

WHAT ARE YOU FEELING?

"You must know what it is to treat it. You must know what your client wants. Anything other than that is about you, not the client."

That was the advice my clinical professor reiterated to me time and time again in training. I never really understood it when I was in training. I was just trying to get the assessment right and identify the different things I had learned in class.

Many times, you see what your client is experiencing, and your insight is so clear. You have the answer and solution. But what if what you see is not what the client wants to be addressed? What do you do?

The Real Symptoms Matter

Imagine going to a deli and ordering a club sandwich only to be delivered a liverwurst sandwich, sauerkraut, and a side of grapefruit. You would be disappointed that the server messed up your order, especially if they had no interest in correcting the order.

Now, imagine if you thought you ordered the club sandwich, but every time the server answered you, they repeated back the incorrect order. That would not only frustrate you, but you would be so confused!

I had one patient in training that I have never forgotten. She was a middle-aged female that came to our clinic because her depression had gotten worse and made it difficult to work. It is an excellent sign for someone to seek treatment, but it often shows the symptoms are getting harder to tolerate. Few people want to go to a stranger and completely bare their soul, especially about their deepest, darkest insecurities.

She sat across from me, somewhat guarded, and appeared a bit suspicious. Honestly, she had every right to be cautious of this fresh-faced young dude in training. I had no idea what I was doing.

As I started the assessment, she described her depression with a vivid picture, highlighting the depth of her suffering. She was hurting, and it showed. I tried to be compassionate and show her that I could help her (even if I doubted myself).

As part of any traditional clinical assessment, you must evaluate any symptoms that may be causing problems. It is common to have several different ailments going on simultaneously, which could complicate the treatment recommendations. Since anxiety and depression are frequent partners, I started to explore feelings of worry, possible panic attacks, and obsessive worries.

Bingo!!!

She began to describe some very detailed obsessional thoughts, mostly about germs, cleanliness, and health safety. Since she worked in health care, it seemed somewhat expected to be concerned about germs in her world.

But it was more profound than that. My patient was so worried about becoming infected with various illnesses that she started to call in sick from work, avoiding going out in public, and spent all day disinfecting her house. (Note – since COVID-19, this may seem healthy, but it is important to note that this happened many years ago.) In my assessment, her increasing depressive symptoms resulted because she was limiting her activity, staying shut in all day long, and not having any positive experiences in her life because of her anxiety.

I felt like a clinical rock star. I had uncovered the issue in record time. I could not wait to share with her the reason for her depression was the negative impact of her obsessive-compulsive disorder (OCD).

I had figured out the reason for emotional suffering. Oh, I was good!

In the interview, although she had described a 30-year history with OCD, she had always been able to stay somewhat functional. She considered her anxiety a minor hassle. She gravitated to her healthcare job because she could clean and be cautious about germs without looking out of line. She had a straightforward level of OCD, and selfishly, that was what made me excited. I wanted to have the chance to treat it.

When I presented her with my treatment plan, I explained to her that while she was depressed, we would collaborate to address her underlying OCD. In doing so, I believed she would start leaving her house more often, and her depression would improve as a secondary effect. I was a freaking genius!

I never saw her again.

She did not show up for her first treatment appointment and later replied that she no longer wanted treatment at all. Her loss, right?

I answered her problems, but I assumed she just did not want to do the work.

My clinical supervisor had asked me how she was doing. I told him that she had declined treatment essentially by never showing up again, and I thought that would be the end of the story. Instead, I got the best professional mentoring ever.

I failed her because I made it about me and not her. She came in for treatment for her depression. Not for her OCD.

The obsessive thoughts had been a part of her entire adult life, and she had managed them just fine. While I was "right" about why her depression had intensified, she did not see the connection. She was hurting and wanted help with the pain from the depression.

I hate that I failed her, but it changed me.

That one clinical experience completely changed how I approached my work and has shaped my overall perspective – focus on what is right in front of you first, and then work on the things in the background. If I had helped her feel better, then maybe she would have wanted to address the underlying issues. Perhaps not, but at least I would have treated her, instead of taking care of my clinical interests.

For many people, some struggle and suffering are okay, so long as expected and understood. The primary concern is the unknown and the potential that things could get worse.

You are no different.

When you are struggling to find your performance stride, you misinterpret what you "feel." Everything mentally and physically feels off, and that disconnection leads to more significant frustration. The symptoms and the cure do not seem congruent. It is easier to bury your head in the sand than face the confusion of the present.

The questions you ask yourself are often more problematic than the struggle itself. Those questions force you to go beyond the immediate moment and stir up long-standing difficulties and insecurities. By trying to look at deeper issues in your struggle, you are digging up deeper wounds.

The internal angst has no equal when mired in a struggle. And it builds on itself.

I bet it seems like your struggles have been getting more complex. They really may be. Or they could be the same, but your response to them has gotten more sensitive.

The most overwhelming part of this challenge is knowing the problem and differentiating your painful reaction to the issues. If you could make that differentiation and figure out exactly what was causing your pain, it would be easier to dig yourself out.

Do not give up.

What you are feeling may be overwhelming and may be getting harder the longer you are stuck in Suckville. I bet you have spent many hours trying to remember where it started or where it worsened, and worse, why this is even happening at all.

Do not waste your time. It has happened. The more you try to understand why the more you stay mired in the past.

The Five Foundational Symptoms

I am going to boil down Suckville into five foundational symptoms. But they are more than just simple signs. They are specific reasons you got stuck in Suckville and why you continue to cause yourself more pain. You must understand what they are and why they have created the mental place you are in at this time. The feelings listed below, alone, are not the issue. It is when they work together and create a changed mental perspective that makes the devastation.

As you read these symptoms, understand them from a larger perspective. View them as adaptable and not fixed. They are not traits like your eye color. Each one has become ingrained in you but can be changed. Knowing you are making these changes can be so contagious in a positive way.

1. Feeling Like You Are Falling Short Of Your Potential

The most vital symptom of Suckville is the continued frustration that your results are falling short of your potential. You look for improvement and believe that you have figured it out, only to get angry and disappointed that your results do not live up to your expectations. Over time, frustration destroys your confidence.

You are not falling short, but you are not producing at the level you believed you could achieve. The frustration builds and builds until you lose all joy and trust in your abilities.

Falling short of a mythical outcome, like your potential, has the same effect as failing at anything. Failing is failing. It hurts, is embarrassing, and causes the same level of frustration as failing at a specific, tangible task.

Frustration is the primary emotion driving Suckville. Frustration is one part disappointment and a whole lot of anger directed inward. As it builds up, it causes more physical and psychological tension. You get more reactive to every struggle, and you magnify every mistake like it is the end of the world.

You want nothing more than to get rid of the frustration. You hope to succeed. You pray to reach your potential, but that possibility seems so far away and out of reach.

When you are training, your skills feel great, and your mind gets excited about the next competition. But practice is not competition. It is more comfortable in practice because the outcome you want so badly is not there. The outcome you want is buried deep in the chaos of the heat of the moment.

"You have so much potential. I don't know why you are falling short," numerous coaches and fans have told you.

"I know I am better than that. I know I can do that," you have told yourself after every disappointing competition.

“I know what I am capable of, and competition is where I can prove it!" is a promise you make yourself.

Throughout the training, you get glimpses of what it could be and romanticize that performance level as the ideal outcome.

Reality is never perfect. The frustration of Suckville makes you think it should be.

Far too often, I come across an athlete who has created a mental framework around being perfect. They become so burdened by the sheer presence of making a mistake that they lose the joy in the competition. Maybe it is because our society is demanding so much more than it ever has, or perhaps it is because competitors can do so much more than ever before. Carrying the standard of PERFECT or fear of SUCK robs the energy from the game. Nothing is ever perfect.

Success is messy, complicated, and volatile. You simply cannot accept anything other than your absolute best. The emotional struggle needs you to be at your best to feel relieved. It is no longer about feeling good, but it is about feeling relief from anger and frustration.

Having a goal or desired outcome is not detrimental to your performance. It is part of the competition. But when you define your joy or happiness based on being at an extreme performance level, you are constantly frustrated.

It did not start like that, though. You made it that way because you started to reject your reality. You got frustrated and started raising the bar.

Things started to be not good enough. You began to validate the level of your training by the quality of your performance. Everything had a contingency associated with it, and your performance continued to fall short.

The more you fixate on your potential, the more you reject your reality. It is never good enough. With each struggle, you get focused on minor areas of struggle as if those difficulties are predictors of a future with constant suffering. Perfection becomes the only acceptable outcome, and you discard your level of performance.

Fixating on the frustrations creates a greater focus on your problems. As you condition your mind to be disturbed by missing your potential, it will find every single reason that struggle exists for you.

Your potential is a mythical concept. It does not exist, and you will never reach it. It is like hunting for the elusive Big Foot. Some signs and signals could exist, but time after time, no evidence exists.

2. Impatience

Growth takes time – lots of it. Success takes even longer. Why are you in such a hurry?

If you accomplish success and reach your potential like you think you should, your level of performance expectation changes. You will never be satisfied.

The player on the team wants to be a starter.

The starter wants to be THE best on the team.

The best on the team wants to be the best in the league.

The best in the league wants to be the best in the region.

The best in the region wants to be the best in the nation.

The best in the nation wants to be the best in the world.

The best in the world wants to be a Hall of Famer.

The Hall of Famer wants to be able to play the game again.

No one is ever satisfied, and it is never happening on the proper schedule.

Why can't it happen faster? You have done the work. But real success does not just take action because of your practice. It takes time to develop into what you want to become.

With each frustration and impatience of your progress, you overlook the smaller pieces starting to line up and come together. With our society's limited attention span and desire for immediate results, you cannot get impatient.

Impatience is a good thing because it is a common trait among elite competitors. If you have trained for the moment, it is customary to want to see the results. Those investments must have a reward.

But why is impatience a symptom of Suckville if the best competitors in the world are impatient?

If impatience drives you to be better and train more effectively, it is good. If impatience spurs you on to have a sense of urgency in competition, then it is effective. But when impatience influences you to reject your progress because it is not happening fast enough, you will reject the truth of your reality. That is when impatience is a problem.

Why would a competitor want to be content and comfortable on the journey to success? Why settle?

Impatience is nothing but doubt attacking your present moment. If you trusted you would eventually succeed, you could wait for the rewards. It may be challenging to be patient, but you would keep doing your job and moving forward.

Impatience intensifies the struggle. It is a constant reminder that you are not where you want to be and not on the correct timeline that creates more significant angst. It motivates greater scrutiny into what you are doing, how you are doing it, and what is missing. Impatience never allows you to come to the immediate conclusion that things are going according to plan.

A little impatience is good. A lot of impatience is terrible. It is a fine line.

The concept of hard work should always be a given and not at the expense of your patience. When you feel you deserve success because of your work ethic, you assume that you control all the other factors associated with your progress.

Do the work, keep your head down, and keep going. Do not fall into the Suckville trap thinking that your hard work makes you unique or deserving. All that does is further widen the gap between your reality and your perceived potential.

Being impatient is simply part of the process. You want success, right?

3. Comparing Yourself to Others

When you focus on the world outside of you, you overlook the world inside you. It is so easy to get distracted by the results of others that you forget your journey.

You must understand the emotions you experience when you observe another having success. Each emotion tells a different story and reflects another aspect of you. Imagine sitting on the sidelines and watching your friends celebrate their championship victory. Now imagine it was after beating you.

Would you feel excited for them? Sure, to a degree. If you have a good relationship with them, you know the effort and sacrifices contributing to their success.

Would you feel disappointed with your result?

Of course! Anytime you are that close to the final goal and fall short, it can only hurt.

Would you be jealous? I think that would be normal because you want what they have and can see yourself in that position. The important distinction is how it impacts your action. If being envious inspires you to work harder, it is healthy. If it inspires you to destroy their joy, it is detrimental.

The primary emotion that ensures Suckville is anger – not at your opponent but at yourself. When you get angry because someone else succeeds, it gets more challenging to work through your struggle. Anger highlights the frustration of continued shortcomings, despite any evidence to the contrary in the present moment.

Anger widens the gap between your current performance level and where you think you should be. When you direct the anger at yourself, you limit yourself because anger redefines what is achievable. You get distracted by the wrong targets or those that are not attainable.

Everyone struggles, but you ignore what it took for them to get there when you only focus on their success. You overlook the periods of their struggle, do not carry the emotional burdens they had to work through or understand their doubts and insecurities to overcome to succeed. All you do is see a snapshot in their journey and use it as ammunition against yourself.

Anger and impatience run together far too often. As you are working towards a goal, the original time plan may have seemed realistic but never according to your timeline. It will always take longer, always be more challenging than you thought, and you constantly question if it is worth it. If you are not asking how long it is taking, you are not fighting hard enough.

There is always an urgency to finish sooner, achieve success faster, and immediately get through the pains. As the struggle continues, your mind speeds up your internal clock. It focuses on those you envy as reminders of how far behind you are. These thoughts only intensify the feelings of Suckville.

4. Resistance to Coaching or Feedback

There is a very distinct difference in how successful competitors accept feedback compared to those who struggle. It amazes me that the more someone struggles, the more resistant they are to being coached and receiving feedback. They become defensive to the helping voices trying to help.

Resistance makes sense when you think about it. When you get stuck in Suckville, your internal voice increases in volume and intensity, making it harder to focus on the right things. Your mind starts spinning faster and faster, and additional information only clutters the message. You lose the ability to filter information and determine the correct path.

Have you ever been lost driving in an area of town late at night in the pouring down rain and were not comfortable?

Did it help to have your passengers try and give you directions simultaneously, with the radio volume turned up?

That is the experience when you are struggling. I have spent hours on driving ranges, in locker rooms, and in coach's offices consoling those stuck in Suckville, trying hard not to add additional information. It is not the right time for more clutter, but instead better information.

When you are stuck in Suckville, it is easy to resist outside influences because you think your success should follow a preconceived pathway. It is easier to resist than push forward.

Not all advice from coaches, teammates, friends, and family will be helpful, even if that advice is phenomenal. Your resistance is not a bad thing.

It is easy to search for quick fixes because they may produce short-term confidence, success, or even a change of overall luck. But those short-term solutions were not implemented for the long haul and lose power, unlike fighting in the immediate moment. Short-term fixes do not build long-term systems of excellence.

When you intend to build excellence, the motivations are always different. You will be more patient with the more minor ups and downs and work through the challenges without making judgments about your progress. You know it will be challenging, but the product will be worth the continued investment.

The challenge is your underlying motivation. If the basis is to fix problems, the motivation is not growth but preserving your current or most recent performance level. Continual fixing of the issues is like patching a roof because of water leaks. In the short term, the patches will work, but the patches will fail over time, and you will have to determine why the roof was leaking in the first place.

Timing also matters. Not all coaching feedback gets delivered at the right time. Coaches get emotional just like players do and often bombard their players with too much information just trying to help them.

It is your responsibility to filter the information and learn to apply it for yourself. You must separate the DATA from the DRAMA of the message. If you get caught up in the drama, you will miss the message. You must find the most important aspects to learn instead of burying yourself in the drama of the moment.

5. Increased Mental Rigidity and Judgment

When struggles intensify, your mind gets more rigid and stubborn. Those who struggle the worst have the most rigid perceptions of their performance, limiting their ability to experience conflict.

Those who are mentally rigid become highly judgmental, and instead of seeing solutions, they only see negative reflections of their limitations. Instead of feeling that there is a way, mentally rigid competitors wonder what went wrong immediately.

In the heat of the moment, the harder it gets, the more your mind wants to overcontrol the moment. As a result, you lose your ability to navigate uncertainty, be innovative, and be creative. You become more judgmental and less mentally flexible.

The judgment you are experiencing through each competition, analysis, and observation of your competitors unravels everything inside you because you can never live up to the standards you set for yourself. It is never good enough, never fast enough, and never your best effort.

Judgment is not about analysis but fear and anger about your progress. You will always fall short and still have more struggles than anticipated. When you add in judgment, you magnify the shortcomings and short-circuit the experience. It simply isn't enough.

You are naturally judgmental, and that has been okay for some time. Even when you are highly confident, you are never pleased. The natural judgment of your performance motivates you to get back to work and strive to be better. People are not wired to be content with progress. It must always be better, or you fail to remain relevant.

The problem arises when your judgment becomes personal, driving a wedge between what you believe you are and your performance level. Who is there to protect you when you attack the details of your effort, training, and competitive experience?

When you ask someone to be honest with you, you probably do not want them to be truthful. You want the feedback to be considerate of your feelings and protect you from the perception of who you are in your mind. You know you have a reality hidden from public view. You are protecting with all your energy, and their honest feedback attacks that dark secret.

But when you are alone, in your head, the gloves come off. It is all about destroying yourself, picking the scabs off the wounds of your emotions, and never letting up. It has its use, but not all the time. It has gotten you out of bed, into the gym, and pushed that extra effort in the past. Imagine playing for a coach who continually beat you down? You would quit.

Your judgment is a misused skill, and when you are struggling, it starts to work against you instead of for you. In Suckville, as frustrations build, your judgmental tone only intensifies, enhancing the painful strikes with surgical precision.

"I suck!"

"I will never break out of this! I have lost my game!"

"I swear, I used to be so good."

And so on. Why does it have to hurt so bad?

Around every aspect of your performance, there is pain and excitement. There are days where it feels fantastic, and there are days where you feel like you're searching for any solution possible in your performance.

What have you done wrong to bring on this pain?

It must be something that you have done wrong. There must be a failure that makes sense.

Emotional variability and competition go together. You will experience a wide range of emotions in the heat of the moment. How you manage your emotional variability is how you separate yourself in competition.

The symptoms of Suckville are the consistencies of struggle and the emotional perspective that you must respond to daily. It wears you down and makes you question if you are strong enough. I have spent time with too many who wonder why they struggle, what is wrong with them, and what their future will look like.

The Cost of Knowledge

The field of athletic performance training has seen a rapid increase in measurement and data analytics over the past decade. Throughout all sports, coaches and performance consultants have driven innovation to identify and understand new contributors to performance success. As a result, athletes can do more, faster.

But at what cost?

The more you know does not always mean the better you will perform. The best will still be the best. The innovation advances have moved the performance standards to more efficient competitors, but I have also watched far too many get lost in the search for performance optimization.

Just because you can measure it does not mean you should be coached or focused on it. You have your style, your psychological fingerprint, that drives your performance growth curve. Far too many have struggled to see improvements fast enough, or with the amount of time, money, and effort invested in their performance. The cost of knowledge many times is increased pressure and reduced mental flexibility.

When you started struggling, you likely reached out for help. You studied your game more. You evaluated every single aspect of your performance and established a plan. But you may have started to pay attention to parts of your game, mechanics, or thought processes that you had never paid attention to in the past. Your awareness and knowledge took away your innocence.

Knowledge does not have to lead to struggle or frustration. You must learn more about your game and performance, but you must do it with an understanding that progress is never according to plan. Getting frustrated and angry about your performance level is not productive. Knowledge is powerful, but only when you use it correctly.

6

TIME TO BREAK THE CYCLE

There was a time the game was fun and innocent for you. When did it suddenly become a burden?

Burden is a harsh word for some competitors. It can be difficult to accept that your relationship with the game may have changed. A true competitor struggles to come to terms with any ending, but when that ending is a changed relationship with the game you used to love, it can be a challenge.

The responsibilities of being an elite competitor bring the pressures to continue performing at an elite level, while for others, the hassles are simply energy suckers. Not everyone comes to despise the game or how the game makes them feel. I have yet to meet a competitor who did not have their relationship get more complicated, however.

I sat on the team bench with a college basketball player struggling with their loss of passion for the game for several hours after a game. She was once an elite recruit who had experienced success in her career. The problem was she no longer enjoyed the "grind" and started to feel the pressure of providing for her extended family. She was the first member of her family to attend college, and her family wanted her to play overseas to financially support them.

She loved the game of basketball, or at least she said that in interviews and discussions.

"Why do you play basketball?" I asked.

"Because it is all I have ever known. I mean, I love it. It is fun. It is my life," she answered.

She loved the idea of playing basketball, but her life was hard. She was confused by her emotions towards basketball and was terrified of letting her family down if she failed overseas. She was not enjoying the freedom on the basketball court anymore. Every game became a test for how she would project as a professional athlete.

Going to the gym became frustrating, practice felt like a chore, and basketball was like an unpaid job. Every day was a job interview for a future but an unknown employer. To make matters worse, she did not even know how she would be evaluated, now or in the future. As a result, her attitude worsened, and she became to loathe the game.

She did love the game in theory and found her identity as an athlete. Her identity was challenged beyond the game, as how she performed determined her self-worth. She was in a downward spiral, a negative cycle, where her self-worth could not be fulfilled simply by great performances anymore. The harder she tried to use success to feel better about herself and her relationships, the worse it got.

The Suckville Cycle

At some point in your competitive journey, you will lose the joy of the game. It happens to every competitor I have ever worked with, and there is nothing you can do to prevent it from happening. Ultimately, the changes in your psychological and emotional engagement with your sport must happen to grow. If you stayed 100% in love with the journey, you would often ignore the opportunities to explore other perspectives or processes. You need apathy to succeed.

Apathy is a psychological state where you experience a lack of motivation or joy in your pursuits. I have always conceptualized apathy as more than just a lack of enjoyment as there needs to be respect for your ability to influence your outcomes. When individuals feel very high levels of apathy, they often feel very powerless to change their circumstances.

Competitors invest so much into their craft that, over time, their efforts start to see reduced outcomes. When the game was fun, the amount you invested in getting better seemed to relate to how much you improved. As the demands and expectations to perform increase, there is greater scrutiny and urgency with those improvements quickly.

You lose the flexibility to figure things out on your own because you feel the need to please someone or struggle to fulfill your expectations. The problem is that you really cannot please anyone else, live up to your expectations, or feel validated because of your work. Those are moving targets. As a result, over time, you start to get increasingly frustrated, eventually to the point of feeling apathetic and helpless.

This is the Suckville Cycle.

Even though you always start with the best intentions, you eventually get broken down by your efforts. You begin to believe you need and can fix every transgression in your game. Those minor improvements are necessary, but not all your performance variances need correcting. When you pursue fixes, all you learn to see are things that need fixing. You never get to focus on what you want to accomplish because you get fixated on constant corrections.

Suckville always begins building before you are even aware that the trouble is brewing. When things are going well and your confidence is high, you abandon the little things that drive success. Your focus starts to shift to other challenges. It's a detail here, a small hassle there, and your effort relaxes. You lose your motivation for the mundane and become infatuated with the new process, new challenge, or time away from the grind.

Then something significant happens.

Your perspective shifts dramatically. The need for constant improvement becomes intoxicating. Those minor corrections start to pile up, and with every failed attempt to eliminate them, you get emotionally worn down. Your competitive focus loses its intensity for delivering success and becomes overwhelmed with the constant reminders of difficulties. The struggles wear you down. This is how Suckville takes over your mindset.

But it is not the struggle itself that is causing your emotional turmoil; you believe that the struggle signals a problem or deficiency in you that is the issue. If you think there is something wrong that is preventing your success, it is natural to try and correct the problem.

I have watched athlete after athlete get lost in the constant journey of self-improvement, only to start hating the game—one more thing to fix, one small change, and another correction here and there.

Those are the promises athletes make to themselves that start the more significant struggles. Challenges make you question your purpose, effort, and perspective, among other things. You need apathy, frustration, and confusion to refocus you on what is most important. From the joy of the game to the burden of the responsibility, the Suckville Cycle happens before you know it. The individual phases progress the same way for every competitor.

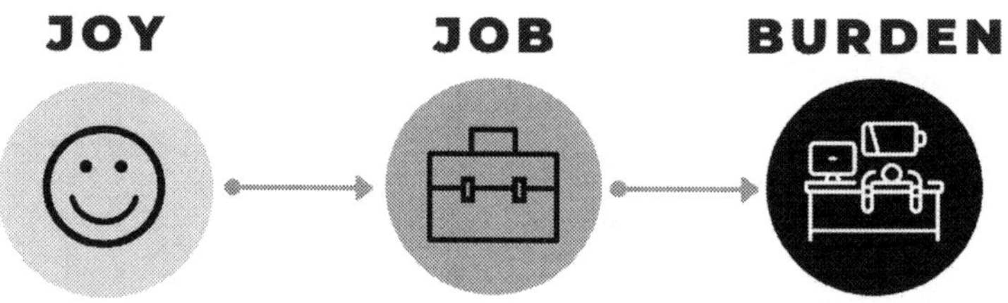

Let me review the three different phases:

1. **When It Was Fun**

I hated to leave the ballpark. The baseball diamond was my playground, which kept me occupied during the early spring days and the long hot summers. It did not matter who I was playing or what team I was on; I just loved to play.

Baseball was special in my family. My dad played college baseball and taught me everything I knew about pitching. He never forced me to practice or overcoached me; instead, he wanted me to love the game as he did. After he got off work, I would beg him to hit fly balls in the backyard until dark. He would take a tennis ball and racquet and hit towering balls into the sky. Before I knew it, there would be ten other neighborhood kids in my backyard catching pop-ups.

My dad and I would listen to baseball games on the radio and shell roasted peanuts. The St. Louis Cardinals were my team (and still are today) and going to games was amazing. I watched with a keen eye, trying to learn everything I could in case I was in the major leagues one day. My lack of talent prevented that from happening, but the joy of the game required no skill.

When I started playing baseball, I wanted to play every possible inning of the game, and it did not matter the position. I would treat every practice as if it were a game and show up with the energy of the championship game. Other players probably hated me, but I loved practice as much as games. Pitching was my thing, and I loved striking guys out.

My journey was not without challenges, but it was fun for the most part. I was never obsessed about getting recruited in high school, probably because I never thought of myself as a college pitcher. Being a part of a team was my goal. As a pitcher, my objective was to get guys out. There was nothing better than striking a hitter out and knowing that you won the battle.

The game is innocent when the objective is clear. You compete for the love of the game and the exhilaration of the competition.

During this phase, hard work produces proportional results, and you correct anything that can be improved with minimal effort. Working on your craft can be pleasurable because you do not expect much in return.

This phase is all about the personal, internal motivations that drive your growth. It is all internal. Growth is fostered by desire and fulfilled by pride.

The rewards are essential to you, but only because of what they mean FOR you. It is not about other people, status, or a scoreboard during this phase. The pursuit of increased competence and mastery in your sport drives your focus.

Challenges are catalysts for learning more about your capabilities during this first phase. With each difficulty worked through, you uncover more about your determination and resilience. The lessons learned tend to be more intrinsically based, connecting the power of your inner spirit with the expression of your abilities.

2. Then It Became a Job

All good things come to an end. The joy of accomplishing a goal eventually dims. Your mind wants more than simplicity and begins to complicate the elegance of the competitive experience.

This phase of the Suckville Cycle represents the shift that happens when your motivations are no longer purely intrinsic. Because of your successes through phase one, you were likely exposed to significant benefits for success. Now, those rewards become the focus of your attention, and that begins the downward spiral.

Accolades.

Access to better players and tournaments.

Attention from outsiders.

Opportunity for a college scholarship.

A contract extension.

You name it; the mind will create it.

When you start to see the benefits of your excellent play, your relationship with the game changes. It is not your fault, though. The benefits of great play are inevitable.

Entitlements begin to foster during this phase. Expectations start to emerge as well. You begin to expect to play great and feel that success is a certainty because of your past successes. Over time, the need to achieve the rewards overshadows the desire to play well simply for you. It becomes a job.

The idea is that if you do the work, then you will receive the benefits. Soon, you begin to need the rewards to do good work. That is why this phase is so volatile. There is a very fine line between playing for you and playing for the rewards. There is no debate that rewards are outstanding, but when you start to expect rewards or need them to be successful, the balance of intention shifts. It is no longer about you but rather what you can get.

Over time, the rewards lose their shine, and you need higher returns on your efforts. You want more and more. When you get what you want, you either start resenting the effort or searching for better ways to perform. You will get increasingly frustrated and exhausted from both scenarios because of the increased efforts without seeing the beneficial returns.

An awakening happens to nearly every collegiate athlete, usually near the end of the first semester of their freshman year, when they realize the amount of work required to succeed athletically in college. All the excitement from the lead-up to attending college gets washed away rather quickly by the difficulty of balancing a full training schedule with a challenging academic load. Young college athletes fatigue quickly and get overwhelmed by the relentless demands on their time.

"This is a job. I used to play because I loved it, now I feel like a full-time employee," is the common sentiment I hear after this awakening. It is not always positive, as many realize the sacrifices are intense for a promised enjoyable experience as a college athlete.

Being a college athlete was an excellent experience for me, but I remember the Friday night team meetings, the Sunday sunrise workouts, and the long bus trips. While I was going through it, the demands seemed brutal. Looking back at that time now, I would love to have one more shot at it again.

The hardest thing for me was trying to fulfill my coach and team's expectations. Every time I stepped on the field, I had a job to do. People were relying on me to get my job done. It was stressful, and for a very distinct period during my senior season, I struggled with those expectations.

When your relationship with the game changes, there is a significant ripple effect. For example,

- *Practice can become a task to be completed instead of a training ground*
- *Mistakes become magnified because you start seeing what you lost due to the mistake*
- *Coaching feedback can start to feel too critical*
- *Your reactions to struggle become more dramatic and judgmental*
- *Pre-competition or performance anxiety builds because of the worry of fulfilling expectations*
- *You start focusing more on the performance of others, fixating on their strengths, and obsessing about your struggles*
- *You become hyperaware of your relationship with your coaches, focusing more on how much they like or dislike you instead of focusing on a player-coach partnership*

When it becomes a total burden to compete, you enter the final phase of the Suckville Cycle.

3. When It Became a Burden

Disney World touts itself as being "The Happiest Place on Earth." For vacationers to have that experience, employees (called cast members by the Walt Disney Company) are critical for delivering that lofty slogan. A bad day for an employee can result in a ruined vacation for a guest. Given the cost of a Disney World vacation, that is a considerable risk for employees.

As a result, Disney World leadership makes a significant financial investment in employee training to ensure the culture delivers on its promise. If you are a member of the Walt Disney Company, they will train you on projecting a positive image and providing a world-class experience for guests. It does not matter the level of your employment either. It is that important to the company.

Imagine if the individual who greeted your family the first morning you arrived at Magic Kingdom, the original park of Disney World, was in a terrible mood, hated their job, and saw the security checks as a burden. Their attitude would not only ruin your day but there is a risk their attitude could negatively influence other employees.

I imagine it must be challenging to be in a great mood every day if you worked at Disney World. It is ultimately a choice you must make – be in a good mood or find another job. I understand how the job could become a burden as I can only imagine the difficulty that tourists can be in the summer heat of central Florida, but employees work very hard not to let it show. But you know it must be a burden.

Those doing the best jobs in the world eventually tire of it. When you first start, you focus on the benefits, salary, and perks of the job, but you begin to realize the areas of frustration over time. There may not be the proper coffee in the coffee room, the hours are too long, or your boss is not supportive enough. The list would go on.

How does that happen?

It occurs when the rewards you receive from competition no longer outweigh the sacrifices you must make to perform at your best. Not only that, but if the rewards are no longer immediate, you will focus on the struggles more than the goodies.

The same thing happens in your competitive journey. What started as fun has become a burden, breaking you down with disappointment, frustration, and exhaustion. Your performances no longer validate your worth. The harder you try only pushes you further away from the possibility of enhanced confidence and happiness.

Your expectations start rising because you are struggling with the level of your performance. Expectations permanently impair performance because they add additional pressure to your intention. Because you will never live up to your expectations, you will start getting more and more frustrated that your performance is not trending the correct way.

Increased expectations led to frustration, not to good play. It is hard to enjoy the game when frustration is present.

The final stage of the Suckville Cycle is when your expectations and subsequent frustration make you feel like everything is a burden. Bad performances are not fun. If you think you cannot change the downward slide of your performances, practice and training will become miserable. Competitions will become painful reminders of what you once had and how far away you feel from that now.

It is tough to compete at your best when you are saddled with frustration and constant disappointment. Those emotions do not inspire hard work but rather foster a feeling of helplessness.

"It does not matter what I do. Nothing seems to work. I put in more time or take time off, neither work. I feel so far away from when things were good. I just suck right now."

That comment describes the final phase perfectly. I hear it day in and day out in my office. It is not a problem that athletes describe their plight this way. I expect it. The worry I have is the helplessness associated with this phase. The more helpless you feel in your journey, the more you seek out anyone to help. That can lead to cluttering the mind with too many quick fixes.

The more helpless you feel in your journey, the more you will doubt that your skills can improve and free you of the struggle. If things did not help yesterday, it is doubtful those same things will help tomorrow.

Apathy and helplessness are similar. If apathy can be constructive to improvements, so can helplessness. When you feel helpless, you are relatively quick to make judgments about the lack of influence your attributes have on changing your circumstances. Because of that judgment, you tend to be very aware of everything you are doing, maybe even hyperaware. You are not lost, just overwhelmed. When feeling helpless, it is very effective to simplify your process and get back to the basics of your performance.

The simplicity is what was fun at the outset. You lost that simplicity because you focused too much on the results and lost the game's innocence. Your journey will become filled with frustration and disappointment the further you go down this cycle, eventually breaking you down emotionally.

When the game becomes a burden, it is a hard place to be. The joy leaves you, and the game becomes a daily reminder of your misery. Most athletes simply want to escape the pain when they get to this point. Whether quitting the game, transferring schools, or counting down the days until the season is over, those solutions only worsen the feelings of the burden. No one wants to compete in an environment where losing is the only option.

You are the way out of the pain.

7

YOU ARE THE GURU

I received a voicemail from one of my top-ranked professional golfers immediately after a tournament. "I finally figured this out. After thirty years in the game, I finally understand a different side of the game. The information was never wrong. I just never found it in what I was taught. I have had it the whole time, but I was never patient enough to let it rise!"

He sent it as he was driving his courtesy car back to the airport, but he could not wait to share his excitement. During the round, he had an awakening, a powerful realization of just how good he was.

For years, he had tried to do precisely what he was taught, to the smallest detail. Every piece of advice and instruction was implemented to perfection. When he struggled, he got so frustrated and would lose ground to the competition.

"If I do not have success and I have all the tools, great coaching, and a locked-in mindset, it must be something wrong with me that is causing me to struggle."

Before the weekend of "awakening," his voicemails were frustrated and angry, often directing that angst at himself. He took all the blame because he believed he was the reason for his struggles as if he was missing something deep inside that the best players in the world had.

As he stood in the middle of the fairway, two shots off the lead during the final round, he challenged himself to "trust me." In the past, as the tension built, he reverted to the practice sessions and coaching moments. It was never about him as the player, always as the student.

That "trust" moment led him to more resiliency and grit on the course. He was more able to accept the good and the bad, and as a result, he had his top finish of the season. His success continued throughout the rest of the season.

When does the student become the master?

When students trust themselves to compete without hesitation, immerse themselves in the uncertainty of the moment, and allow ultimate vulnerability, they discover their master within. It is never about the information but always the implementation.

Who Are You?

You are a work in progress. When you were born, you were gifted with the ability to face unique opportunities and endure tremendous challenges in your life. There was no user's manual that came with you and no guide map for your future. You had to figure out what you had inside you to face the multitude of challenges bombarding you from the outside.

How do you know what you have inside until you challenge your true abilities? The traits and talents you have learned to trust are only the tip of the iceberg. There is so much more to you than you can ever understand.

A dynamic relationship between your genetic portfolio and the critical experiences of your life, those times when you had to dig so deep just to persevere, formed the psychological framework you have today. You cannot do much about those traits from your parents, as it is hard to change the hand you write with and your overall temperament. Those are stable and take a significant amount of work to change those hardwired instincts.

The combination of your genetic traits and your experiences create a unique mental framework, what I refer to as your "psychological fingerprint." Your learnings and experiences mold around your stable characteristics, creating a framework that you use to respond to challenges and opportunities. Your psychological fingerprint gets tested with each challenge, resulting in changes and refinements as you mature. It does not become more effective unless you are tested.

Many of the stable traits seem to get confused with correctable things. While many coaches get frustrated by the quick and volatile emotions of certain players, they fail to recognize the near automatic nature of those reactions. It is deeper than "trying" to not be emotional. It is who they are.

I get calls all the time about a player's response when competing and the problems it seems to cause. The parent does not realize that they display the same behavior that they want their athlete to change when they call me. It is like they are related!

I evaluate the player's disposition, mindset, and resilience that form their psychological fingerprint from a wide angle. As a clinical psychologist as my professional foundation, I rely on a psychological framework – the BioPsychoSocial Perspective – that I have used across many different patient groups, with a wide variety of conditions. The perspective allows me to see their uniqueness without getting distracted by glaring difficulties.

First formulated and published in 1977 by Psychiatrist George Engel, the BioPsychoSocial Perspective emerged from his own clinical experiences with varying levels of health and illness. For years prior, it was common practice for practitioners to conceptualize illness as either a born-in trait or something directly related to the patient's experience. The BioPsychoSocial Perspective shifted thinking to see health and illness as genuinely personal.

The BioPsychoSocial Perspective has helped me appreciate how a person's underlying biology or genetics interact with their psychological processes throughout various social settings. It is never one thing or the other, but a combination of many things which makes your psychological fingerprint unique.

For instance, here are a few differences that highlight the uniqueness based on setting:

- *Does your confidence differ between settings, like school, sports, and social settings?*
- *Are you more aggressive in one aspect of life and more cautious in another?*
- *Is it easier to accept feedback from a teacher but not a coach?*
- *Are there areas in your life that you are patient and other areas that you quit as soon as it gets hard?*

Below is a brief primer on the Biopsychosocial Perspective that contributes to the development of your psychological fingerprint.

BIOLOGICAL FACTORS

GENETICS
We are born different and hold different capacities and attributes. What do they have the capacity for?

SPORTS SPECIFIC FACTORS
Factors such as handedness, reaction time, and sport skill, that are coachable, have a biological component.

MEDICAL/INJURY HISTORY
Medical limitations and injury history can showcase or strengthen physiological factors.

PSYCHOLOGICAL SCREENINGS/LIMITATIONS
Functional limitations are important to know if the player is capable of competing.

PARENTAL ATHLETIC HISTORY
How do their parents coach and model behavior?

PSYCHOLOGICAL FACTORS

MOTIVATION
What motivates the player? Achievement? Avoidance? Acceptance?

VISION OF THE FUTURE
Where do they see themselves in 4-6 years?

SELF-EFFICACY
Level they believe that they can succeed at the task.

HANDLING PRESSURE
Under pressure, do they respond to challenge aggressively or tentatively?

VULNERABILITY
Are they willing to accept the outcome?

SPIRITUAL/EMOTIONAL BALANCE
How do they cope?

RESILIENCY
How do they bounce back from disappointment?

SOCIAL FACTORS

COACHABILITY
Do they handle coaching? What type of coaching is best for them?

ACCEPTANCE OF RESPONSIBILITY
Easy to transfer the blame but can they take responsibility for actions?

SOCIAL SUPPORT
Who do they perceive as supporting them?

PLANS FOR IMPROVEMENT
What is the process or plan to achieve goals and desires?

There is no right or wrong personality or psychological fingerprint. I have yet to find a particular psychological fingerprint that tells me specifically if a player can succeed with certainty. All that matters is how they learn to trust their psychological fingerprint in training settings, stressful competitions, and moments when things get complicated.

You do not have to be calm to be good. You do not have to be intense to be successful. Being aggressive only matters if you learn to do that every time. It is about knowing who you are.

No One Knows You Like You Do

You are the guru in your game and life. No one else has the answer for you when you are in the heat of the moment. No one sees through your eyes and experiences what you experience. It is your experience, so own it fully.

It is a tragic mistake to tell a competitor what they should be thinking, doing, and experiencing in the heat of the moment. As a competitor, you need to embrace the uniqueness of your psychological fingerprint and learn the limits, strengths, and shortcomings. When outsiders attempt to tell you how you should behave and think, they take your psychological fingerprint for granted.

Stop trying to play the way others want you to. Steve Jobs, the brilliant innovator and driving force behind Apple, understood the greatest lesson of every great leader – do what you think you should do, not what others think you should do. For you to be your best, you must reconnect to your authentic self. I can guarantee that you do not even remember who that is.

When the game is over, and your career fades into the sunset, do you want to look back and wish you had done it your way?

Or do you want to look back and think you should have listened to outsiders more?

Win or lose, success or failure, do it the way you know how to, for you. Work within the team, listen to your coaches and translate their messages into your language. As former American Idol judge Randy Jackson famously told aspiring artists, "Make it yours, Dawg."

Each time you are in the heat of the moment, you can learn more about who you are and how you compete. Do not waste those opportunities to know more about your psychological fingerprint.

The most challenging circumstances in your life reveal and sharpen your underlying psychological strengths. With each success, you learn more about successful perspectives. With each failure, you eliminate those that cause additional problems.

I never want a competitor to mimic another, even the world's best players. You are so unique that you must learn about the authenticity of your psychological fingerprint. Trying to change who you are at the core of your competitive psychology is like changing positions or teams and not knowing the plays.

Do not be like Tiger Woods.

Do not try to think like Diana Taurasi.

Do not focus like Katie Ledecky.

Be you.

That is phenomenal enough.

I had two clients in back-to-back coaching sessions that could not have been anymore different. One was an All-American defensive lineman on the football team, and the other was an Olympic hopeful on the diving team. The defensive lineman walked in and started talking about breaking down game film to optimize his performance and gain an edge on his opponents. He noticed that on his best plays, his technique never varied. Based on that, he started focusing on his technique to be able to trust it in the highest-pressure moments.

He wanted to control what he could control in each play, which boiled down to quieting his mind and focusing on his technique. He avoided trash talk in the game and never tried to get hyped before a game. He was a tactician. At night, he would study the technique of professional players and tried to understand their motives. He was the ultimate craftsman.

In the next appointment, the diver reflected on feeling power on the platform, and when she focused on the mechanics of her style, she slowed down and struggled to execute. She loved hype music and would dance on the pool deck before her dives. She did not like it when a coach tried to pump her up because she was already there. The competition was like a dramatic performance, not a tactical demonstration.

She had learned that when her energy was high, she could flawlessly execute her dives. Her video review focused more on the elegance of diving and not the technique. She did not even follow Olympic divers on social media or know the legends in her sport. She knew more Hip-Hop artists than athletes.

While the two athletes were different in so many ways, their unique approaches to breaking down their performances were so diverse that it shocked me. The only commonality they possessed was that their coaches were trying to change how they approached their craft in the highest-pressure moments. They each had their psychological fingerprint and understood how it could drive elite performances.

Both continue to have incredible success in their sport. The elegance of the unique approaches defined the concept of a psychological fingerprint. Each learned what their competitive personalities were, and in doing so, began to appreciate their psychological fingerprints. My job was to shine a light on their assets instead of trying to squash their approaches. Even though coaches wanted to change them, my goal was to bring out what made them phenomenal.

Be You.

Learn who you are and start to embrace it.

I have found that there are several different personalities competitors rely on when the pressure gets intense. Certain competitors know how they prefer to approach the heat of the moment because of the years of refining their approach. Others, unfortunately, are all over the spectrum with limited internal guidance. Those who struggle tend to serendipitously find their personality about 20% of the time and play well. All the factors seem to align with the optimal mindset effectively, but the other 80% worries me.

I never want competitors to leave potential success up to factors beyond their awareness, so it is essential to learn how you function best in the heat of the moment.

Here are my different competitive personalities that contribute to the various psychological fingerprints, so use this to discover who you are, so you can trust yourself when it matters.

Competitive Personalities

1. The Energy Player

In full disclosure, I was an Energy Player. I needed lots of energy to play my best. I thrived when the other team would start talking trash because it gave me something to focus on rather than worrying about my mechanics. I loved coming in relief in the most significant moments of the game to get the team out of a contentious situation. The more drama and pressure made it better for me.

I struggled when I was the starting pitcher or had to pitch in a blowout when there was not much intensity left. The reason may shock you – when the energy was low, I could hear my doubts more. When my mind got quiet, my insecurities became louder.

The Energy Player must learn how to raise their internal arousal or excitement level, despite the presence of any external circumstances. If you enjoy talking or play better when trying to destroy your friends, this may be the position for you. If you thrive off trash talk, use that energy to focus on the moment.

As an Energy Player, you need to take the time to elevate your energy before you compete. It may be the use of hype music or find a way to get a chip on your shoulder. Feeling like you are the underdog or that people do not respect you can help you get more focused, intentional, and aggressive. To get your energy dialed in, you must know your pre-competition routine and give yourself the time to lock in.

An energy player rarely gets too elevated; instead, they limit themselves to feel the way they desire. It is no one else's responsibility to dial in the energy, so find the time to get locked in.

You see many examples of Energy Players in sports because they tend to express their energy through their body language or behavior. The most important caveat is to remain disciplined and not lose your approach because of high energy. Some examples of Energy Players from what I can observe:

- Michael Jordan, basketball – he found a way to get a chip on his shoulder that others did not believe in him.

- Max Scherzer, baseball – he pitches with tremendous intensity and will find ways to amp it up before he pitches between hitters.

- Serena Williams, tennis – she seems to thrive when others doubt her or her back is against the wall.

- Fernando Tatis, Jr, baseball – he is ushering in a new era in the game. With high energy celebrations and prolific home runs, Tatis feeds off the energy of the game.

- Tiger Woods, golf – he would often get angry and use that energy to focus, as he was never scared to show his emotions because they helped him.

- Conor McGregor, MMA fighter - a mixed martial arts fighter, McGregor excites himself to train with the intensity that is only matched when he steps in the ring.

2. The Tactician

You often hear The Tactician referred to as a cerebral player, a very thoughtful and calm performer. What you do not see is how they feel underneath. Players that fall into this competitive mindset category rely on systematic, process-based actions to meet every demand. It does not matter what is going on around them if they can do what they do every time. Their processes are refined in practice and trusted when it matters.

If you are a Tactician, your approach may center around your technique, game strategy, or mental procedure. My defensive lineman loved to focus on his footwork and hand position at the snap. That was the only place he tried to focus. He believed getting set against the ground with his hands solidly in front of him provided a solid base to take on the opponent. Before each snap, he focused on his foot movement and then visualized the placement of his hands. That was all he focused on before the snap. It was tactical from the outset. The bigger the moment, the more he focused on his steps and hand position.

Tacticians use their pre-competition arousal or anxiety to focus on what they can control – their process. It is their recipe, their secret. The best tacticians could give you a seminar on the intricate side of the game and break down each element as if they have been in the game for 50 years. It is what feeds them.

Tony Gwynn was one of the purest hitters in the history of Major League Baseball. He was a throwback player who was probably better suited for the game in the 1950s as he focused on working pitching counts and driving singles. Home runs would come but were never a part of the game for Gwynn. As a Hall of Fame player, Gwynn won each at-bat due to his detailed scouting reports of opposing pitchers, studying their tendencies with fevered energy. By the time he stepped into the batter's box, he had already won the at-bat.

Gwynn was a Tactician. His process was his genius. If you thrive in competition because of your tactical perspective, take the time to build that mindset before you compete. You do not have to get hype or calm down; just focus on the procedural steps to dominate.

Other Tacticians are:

- Bryson DeChambeau, golf – he has committed to his unique process to win a US Open.
- Katie Ledecky, swimming – her process is unique to her competitors but results in dominating performances.
- Mike Trout, baseball – Trout has continually performed at an elite level but with a business-like approach.
- Lewis Hamilton, racing – a complete professional tactician that becomes one with the car and tactically manages the track.
- Sue Bird, basketball – has total control of the court, distributes the ball evenly, and does so with a stoic presence.

3. The Chameleon Player

One of my elite professional athletes can be very intense at times and very tactical in others. She can rely on the hype of playing in front of massive crowds to fuel her drive and, during other times, become so focused on one technical aspect of her game that her mind appears blank. As one of the world's top-ranked players, her approach is a perfect balance between The Energy Player and the Tactician, leading me to conceptualize players like her as Chameleon Players.

Players who can summons whatever it takes mentally to meet the demand in front of them, find a way to become what they need to become to compete just for that specific challenge. It does not matter what is happening around them; all that matters is that they do what it takes to rise to the challenge in front of them. It is their inside process meeting the demand of the external uncertainty. By becoming a chameleon, they are more connected to who they are and more accepting of the good and the bad because what matters is meeting the demand.

If you are a Chameleon Player, trust you have a multitude of different ways to compete. Think of it like alter egos, and in competition, you have a team of various competitors to call on to get the job done. One is not better than the others, as each constitutes a particular mental focus.

The most important thing about being a Chameleon Player is to allow yourself the mental flexibility to adapt and adjust as you draw that unique mindset to meet the demand. You do not try and call it back up tomorrow; instead, you take what you have tomorrow and own it from there. Every day is a new challenge, and every challenge is a unique opportunity to compete as necessary to meet the challenge right in front of you.

Because players in this category are a chameleon, it is hard to be confident who they are, but here are a few thoughts:

- Dustin Johnson, golf – as the 2020 Masters champion, Johnson has the unique ability to channel his energy into improved play at times and, in others, focus on a specific technical key to help him perform. I have walked several practice rounds with him, and it is always intriguing to eavesdrop on his conversations describing his process. It is more systematic than you may think.

- Steph Curry, basketball – arguably the greatest shooter in basketball history, Curry has a comprehensive training plan for each day, yet can surge off the moments in a game.

- Yadier Molina, baseball – catchers are typically game managers, calling pitches, and leading the team, but Molina is also the energy of his team, celebrating great plays and exciting himself to deliver when it matters.

- Michael Phelps, swimming – the greatest swimmer of all-time, Phelps was technically superior and could win races with strategic game plans, but also fed off other swimmers wanting to beat him.

4. The Worrier

I used to play baseball with a teammate who would get so nervous before every game that he would have intense gastrointestinal problems leading up to the first pitch. He would lay down on the bench and eat Pepto Bismol like it was candy. You did not want to sit anywhere near him! As soon as the game started, it would go away (if he could make it to his position without issues).

He would worry about the pitcher, the umpires, the outcome of the game, everything. Nothing could curb his worry other than letting him talk things out.

Every. Single. Game.

The peculiarity was that he was a superstar and played over a decade in Major League Baseball. He did not worry about other parts of his life, but he had to worry about feeling ready when it came to being locked in on the game. His worry was a way he eventually focused on the game.

Some players must play out the worst-case scenarios in their heads to be ready. Once they work through each negative outcome, they relax and realize that they are prepared to handle anything. It can be exhausting for the player, but they cannot let go of the worries without going through them.

Worriers do their best when they take the time to record or journal their apprehensions leading into an event. By seeing them on paper and getting them out of their minds, the worries turn to full conviction to compete. The anxiety turns to action. If you are a Worrier, be disciplined in your recording process to see the things you are stressing about concretely. Take the time before you compete, or better yet before you even head to the competition.

Worriers can be very hard to recognize unless you are in their inner circle. Instead of identifying specific athletes that are Worriers, here are some things you may see:

- ***Hyperactivity*** – highly anxious players may have a difficult time sitting down before a competition. They may pace around the locker room, have difficulty sitting still, or be highly talkative.

- ***Negative Focus*** – Worriers share the adverse risks more commonly than positive opportunities throughout the competition. It is not necessarily bad, just where their focus is directed.

- ***Physical Symptoms*** – nausea/vomiting, upset stomach, or difficulty eating before competitions. I am not talking about a little bit of difficulty because Worriers have significant issues before they compete.

5. The Let Go – Let God Player

I always wanted to be the player who could simply "let go" in competition. Even today, giving talks or writing, I use energy to produce content. I have been fascinated by competitors who can give everything they have, and regardless of the outcome, just go about their business. You cannot tell if they had a good day or a bad day.

I ran into a player who I consider a Let Go-Let God Player. Even though he is not a client, I have spent significant time around him to know how he functions. I asked him how he can let go in the most significant moments. His answer was simple – "What else do I need to worry about right now? The work is done. It is time to let go." So simple, yet difficult for so many.

If you are a Let Go-Let God Player, control what you can and fully accept that the outcome does not influence your self-image. Results are simply the end of a competition, not a mandate on your capabilities. It can be helpful to compartmentalize performance in that matter.

What else do you have to control? Nothing because the outcome is more significant than you, and a competitive outcome can never create your self-image. Your power comes in keeping your self-image separate from your successes. You can be emotional, excitable, and driven to succeed but keep everything in perspective. If this personality is your style, focus on the bigger picture and then set your energy on the immediate task at hand. Let Go-Let God Players of attention are:

- Webb Simpson, golf – the former US Open and The Players' Champion has a remarkable ability to flow between the good and bad without much of a difference.

- Barry Sanders, football – the Hall of Fame running back played with a freedom on the field that allowed him to be a workhorse in the league for many seasons.

- Simone Biles, gymnastics – her focus has been on pushing the limits of gymnastics, but her execution level seems to rise when she competes. It appears that she does the hard work in training and allows herself to put on a show in competitions. Despite her troubles in the 2020 Olympic Games (in 2021 due to COVID-19), she was able to return and compete on the balance beam, earning a bronze medal.

Ultimately, it is your responsibility to learn who you are and what you like about your competitive mindset. The most significant conflict comes when you get coached out of your style. You fall into the trap of listening to outsiders because they seem to do it better, or you have made them into an expert. But they are not the expert of you. You are.

You are unique for so many reasons. Your interaction with the world is all you. No one can own that experience for you, and no one can make it harder or more comfortable. They are nothing more than influences. The years of growth and development have provided you with the opportunity to refine your psychological fingerprint application.

Your psychological fingerprint is unique to you. Through success and struggle, you learn to know who you are. It becomes the ultimate gift to know who you are so you can share with others.

While your physical fingerprint does not change over time, you gain understanding by impacting others, working through challenges, and overcoming obstacles. Stop looking at others with envy and start looking at yourself with amazement. No matter how hard it is right now, I bet if you looked at your circumstances from a 30,000-foot view, you would see so many aspects of yourself with pride and joy. It may be challenging right now, but you are learning more and more about yourself.

Take a step back and appreciate all that you have accomplished to even be in this position. You have earned the right to struggle. If you had not advanced to the level of performance you are at today, you would not have had to learn more about yourself. Right NOW is the most critical time of your life. It is time to change your perspective.

You are the ultimate guru. Start acting like it!

8

YOUR FORMULA FOR SUCCESS

Professional sports franchises have modified their scouting departments to embrace data analytics, statistical modeling, and even nontraditional performance assessments in recent years. The reason is apparent – it is tough to predict who will succeed at the professional level.

Imagine the challenge of being a general manager of a professional sports franchise and having to predict the level of performance for your draft pick or free agent signings based upon nothing more than intuition. Sure, you could identify specific predictors that you feel are important, but most of them would be nothing more than fancy fortune-telling or good luck charms. For every success, there are probably a few close misses and even more complete failures. But the power of hitting it on the mark is incredible.

A couple of years ago, I had a meeting with a Player Personnel Director of an NFL franchise. His role within the franchise was to identify and select talent through the draft and free-agent market. He had a diverse background with experience in just about every American enterprise sector, from military to business to education. When it came to identifying the next superstar, he was stumped. It was even harder to determine who would fail altogether.

Can you imagine the responsibility and long-term cost of missing a prospect?

It is even worse when your franchise's prospect missed and a player you overlooked ends up succeeding. Tom Brady, the future Hall of Fame quarterback of the New England Patriots, and in 2020 the Tampa Bay Buccaneers, was overlooked by every NFL team for five rounds. Eventually, the Patriots drafted Brady with the 199th pick, a 6th round selection. Although he was not considered a franchise quarterback in the pre-draft lead-up, his eventual draft position was shocking as he was the 7th quarterback selected. By the time Brady retires, he will have earned nearly $300 million in salary and at least six Super Bowl victories. The other quarterbacks in that draft struggled in the league and did not last.

How could NFL executives miss so badly? What were they overlooking in Tom Brady, and what intangibles were they focused on that led them to select the other quarterbacks? For some of the executives, it cost them their jobs.

The answer lies in a complex human performance model in which no one knows what predicts success. Researchers, executives, politicians, and military leaders have invested so much in studying it, only to answer, "it depends," or "it is complicated." Success is not predictable.

But you can prepare for success.

While it may be difficult to predict success, it is easier to identify what sabotages success. You could assume factors would risk success like ineffective training strategies, external distractions, poor nutrition, technical limitations, and injuries. However, if you get embroiled in the risks, you will ignore your differences to optimize your performance.

The Success Formula

Your success is a formula, one that embraces your unique individual contributions and requires you to respond to external factors beyond your control. Your triumphs do not happen by chance. The Success Formula increases the probabilities of success in your favor.

Over time, the contributing factors driving your success continue to optimize for consistent production. Just think of great athletes or teams who have consistent success. Outsiders think they are lucky, get all the right calls, or get the best opportunities. Still, the truth lies in refining their process and optimizing their individualized formula for success. No one was simply born successful. The best competitors leverage their Success Formula time and time again.

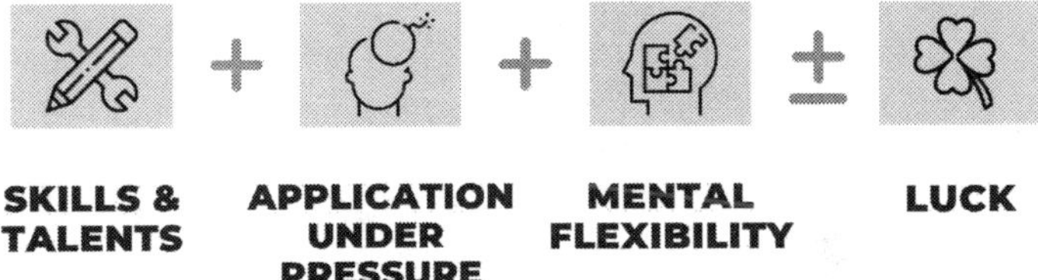

1. Talent

You were born with a set of skills unique to you. Throughout your early developmental years, particular abilities were refined, and others were abandoned. You still know how to crawl, but you are a much better walker and runner than when you were 24 months old. You have adapted and improved your skills through trial and error.

Over time, your talents and skills have improved to meet the opportunities and challenges in your developing life. Each challenge forces you to apply your abilities, and they get better with each application. You need friction and resistance to improve your skills. They simply do not improve with smooth pathways.

The concept of "talent" has been at the center of academic research and applied sciences for several decades. It is a fascinating debate and one that authors such as Daniel Coyle, Robert Greene, David Epstein, and Anders Erickson have explored for decades. Through it all, there are things that specific individuals do better than others. Some of this appears to be genetic.

I was in college with Shaquille O'Neal at LSU. Towering at 7 feet and 1 inch tall, he could move in space better than any post player I had ever seen. He carried his enormous size on his physical frame like a six-foot-tall point guard. The fact that he was seven feet tall was a genetic gift. But he had other talents that he refined. Shaq evolved from a defensive specialist to a professional basketball Hall of Famer. Talent started the process.

I remember being in the weight room, and Shaq would come in to work on specific movements. When many strength workouts were generic, Shaq's were built for his unique skill set in order maximize his size and speed in the post. His coaches took his talents and refined them, making his development around his very advantageous speed, unique among many players his size.

My college roommate was a future 12-year-Major League baseball player, Todd Walker. He had the best hand-eye coordination that I had ever seen. He was not physically intimidating and not super-fast. Still, his ability to maximize hand-eye coordination made him a multiple-time All-American, College Baseball Hall of Famer, 1st Round pick in Major League baseball, and unanimously the best college baseball 2nd baseman ever. He was talented and gifted. But he did not come from a home of great baseball players.

When Todd moved in, he brought a computer station and set it up in his room. In the early 1990s, a computer was not small or fashionable, but Todd's computer had different attachments. His computer station was a hand-eye coordination training system, with foot and hand pedals attached to this computer. He would sit and challenge himself on the computer each night, testing his hand-eye coordination like it was a championship game.

Talent refined.

Watching both Todd and Shaq in college, they took their talents and refined them into elite skills. Many have talent, but a large proportion leave skills on the table because they do not take it to the next step – skill acquisition.

Just because a coach tells you that you are talented does not mean that you will be successful. You must develop those talents into skills.

You have talent. No one is devoid of abilities. You simply must learn what you can do with it.

I knew I would not be the best ballet dancer simply because I lacked the grace and nimbleness to be an expert, not to mention rhythm and flexibility. But my dad was an athlete, specifically a baseball player through college. I am sure that I had some talent to perform at the level I did, but I also had his knowledge to refine those talents into skills.

2. Application Under Pressure

Millions of social media posts highlight the tremendous athletic abilities of athletes all over the world. You do not see how they were created with editing, staging, and controlled conditions.

While it looks great to throw a baseball 100 mph, hit a massive drive on the driving range, or even sing in your living room, it is an entirely different game under the brightest lights. As the pressure intensifies, so do your thoughts, your tension, and your risk of consequences.

The best of the best executes under the most significant moments of pressure.

Serena Williams.

Mariano Rivera.

Steph Curry.

Tiger Woods.

Lindsey Vonn.

Michael Phelps.

U2.

Michael Jordan.

Allyson Felix.

And so on.

You must learn to perform in front of the most intense audiences. With each success, the pressure builds. The heat of the moment is different from every other time you compete. It is not practice, training, or fun.

It is chaos.

It changes your thought process and your approach to the game.

You were not born ready to compete in front of large crowds, immense pressure, and with significant consequences. Your level of success is determined by how you use your skills and talent under pressure.

Your mind cannot calm down the pressure and intensity in the moment. The only thing that quiets the noise is experience—tons of it.

When the moment intensifies, chaos takes over every aspect of your mental and physical functioning. You experience racing thoughts, increased pounding in your heart, a dry mouth, and a complete loss of time awareness. Everything speeds up while you simply want everything to slow down.

Pressure is not the enemy, nor does it discriminate. It is hard to perform without any stress. You need your heart rate to get elevated and your mind to get tunnel vision to optimize your focus. Increased intensity in the moment comes down to understanding how it impacts you.

The pressure of the moment comes from a variety of contributing factors. From the first game of the season to the championship match, there is pressure. Anytime there is a desire to perform at a certain level in the face of consequences, pressure elevates. There may be an element of social acceptance, personal validation, or intense desire that increases the urgency to perform at a level you desperately want. That is pressure.

Pressure reveals who you are at the core. It is an equal opportunity offender. Pressure does not care about your talent level, how many people support you, or your social media following. It is coming for you, and it does not apologize.

What you gain from experiencing pressure is up to you. If you do not appreciate it and learn from it, you are doomed to repeat the pains. The intensity of pressure is never enjoyable in the moment, but the lessons can create pleasurable memories.

Pressure impacts every competitor across four distinct domains – Physical, Psychological, Decision Making, and Resiliency.

- ***Physical:*** Increased pressure can change the mechanical and physical execution of your skillset. Sometimes, you may get too quick in your movements, and other times, you may get more protective and deliberate. The important thing is to understand what changes pressure creates in your physical execution. It is unique to you.

- ***Psychological:*** As the pressure builds, your mind must prepare you for the potential challenge. It does not do that by feeling relaxed and quieting down. Your mind responds as if it were anticipating threat and danger. As a result, you may have trouble concentrating, focusing, and slowing down your thoughts. Negative thoughts increase when under pressure as well. Your relationship with pressure will demonstrate a unique interaction with the psychological side of performance. One way is not the right or wrong way. It is specific to you.

- ***Decision Making:*** I always find how competitors make complex decisions in the heat of the moment to be inspiring. Tiger Woods, one of the greatest golfers to play the game, could execute with absolute precision with the world watching every shot. He told a professional client of mine that his secret to managing pressure was his decision-making. Competitors would get too aggressive or feel that they had to perform better than their average when matched against him, so Tiger simplified his approach. In doing so, he let competitors make the mistakes he knew they would make and keep a stress-free perspective to his own game. It was not a conservative game plan, but he wanted to take very few risks and leverage his strengths. His strengths were what he could trust the most, and under pressure, he did not want to rely on complicated aspects of his game.

- ***Resilience:*** When pressure mounts, your ability to stick with the process is essential. It is common to hold back effort because you are concerned that things will not go your way, even harder when success is not guaranteed. Far too often, I have found competitors subconsciously hold something back in the most challenging circumstances. I am not sure if holding back is protection against being fully vulnerable or if it is easy to justify failing if you knew you had more in the tank to give. That is the universal question that I have been trying to solve for many years, but this phenomenon is so common that I must understand it more. Everyone has that quit moment when pressure builds, so you must learn how the intensity of volatile competition impacts your resilience and grittiness.

3. Mental (Psychological) Flexibility

Mental or psychological flexibility is the most critical developmental psychological skill I have observed among the most successful competitors. In the heat of the moment, the increased pressure intensifies the clutter, drama, and trauma in such a way that you must learn to adapt and overcome. When you mix the internal mental challenges with the enhanced uncertainty of competition, the best competitors embody a mental fluidity to work through challenges. You cannot do that if you get stuck in a singular way of thinking.

As chaos intensifies, you risk getting more judgmental of your actions and results. It is not personal. It is protective, even if it is not helpful in competition. You get more judgmental for a simple reason – to protect against more struggle. When you get more judgmental, you draw your attention to the negative experiences to manage those troubles. The problem with this focus is that it does not work because you overreact to your experiences.

Your ability to mentally adapt to the challenges shows you that you have more effective skills than you initially believed. What ultimately matters is your depth of expertise and the application of that expertise to push through challenges.

Great competitors maximize their mental flexibility by pivoting away from the struggle and refocusing their attention on the most pressing purpose in the competition. It is not about resisting or avoiding, but instead dancing with the dangers and leading through them.

Good and bad will happen. You cannot build your mental game around the good and hope the negative never occurs. That mindset will only leave you exposed to the reality of competition.

The chaos of competition makes things hard, but you are better than any difficulty you will encounter.

You may not need all the tools in your toolbox. Each circumstance requires different solutions. The important point about being mentally flexible is not necessarily about the specific skill you utilized but rather that you could meet that demand. With each experience, your mastery of facing the challenge becomes better, and you build a better toolbox.

Mental flexibility must become your superpower. It is up to you to understand, appreciate, and respond to what is happening in your life. With increasing pressure associated with the uncertainty of all competition, your ability to adapt becomes critical.

4. Luck

You cannot ever control what happens to you. In 2020, a novel coronavirus, COVID-19, impacted our country and the world, disrupting the economy, social activities, and overall health and wellness. It will take years to recover.

It happened. The virus and subsequent decisions were unprecedented.

Competition is never guaranteed to follow a particular strategy. Good things will happen to you. Bad things will happen at other times. You may get injured, and you may stay healthy. For the most part, the outcome is out of your control.

You may be able to influence whether you win or lose, but more factors, some even mysterious, demand your attention that turns the course of the competition. Many vague factors bombard your focus and attention that it is often hard to determine the real reason for the outcome.

All that matters is how you mentally and physically face uncertainty. You have the skills and tools to work through it. The outcome may not be ideal but walking away is never as good as trying and working through it. It is up to you to manage the volatile nature of your journey.

The challenge with luck is that you must accept the limits of your influence. Despite all you do, there is so much more beyond your control. Giving up a sense of control can be very difficult, but you can succeed if you have optimized the Success Formula's other factors.

Luck also leverages one additional element – your emotional influence. More so, your emotional reactions to what is happening to you. Without emotion, the randomness of your competitive life would be nothing more than simple experiences in the background, like cars driving by you on the interstate. It is never that straightforward, hence, why your emotional or mental flexibility is so important.

Each random experience attaches to the emotions in your memory and makes projections about your future. Everything represents something. The more something is, the more emotions are centered on it.

For instance, a referee's lousy call may be a random occurrence, but if you are mired in a slump of epic proportions, that bad call is equivalent to one more powerful reminder that the game is out to get you.

"I cannot buy a break. The game hates me," I have heard numerous times.

I have said it too.

The problem with luck and emotion is that you see good luck differently when you are having success. You fall into the trap that good events are always because of your abilities. That erroneous conclusion is the heart of the problem.

Random events that go against you, or bad luck, are confirmation that the game is beating you. It is bad luck after bad luck, making it harder and harder for you to succeed. The power of those events is massive. When you are highly confident, however, those random events are confirmation of your elite skill. The ball gives you a great bounce becomes a sign that you are in the right frame of mind.

Random outcomes or just plain luck are nothing more than that. As you attach your emotion, you make it personal. That is the problem that must be separated.

The Secret Sauce – The Belief Ladder

The Success Formula lays out the standards of what it takes to succeed through each layer of struggle that you may experience. But what if you do everything in your power and still struggle?

One of the most common sentiments I receive from players is when they feel they are doing everything they trained for and still struggle.

"I should be better than that" becomes the common descriptor for less-than-ideal performances.

"With the amount of training I am putting in, things should be better than this!"

"I work harder than everyone else. Why do my competitors succeed, and I continue to come up short?"

If the Success Formula is definitive, players should never fall short.

But there is a secret element driving the most incredible athletes – BELIEF. It is not a genetic trait, nor is it a personality. It is learned and earned.

I would argue that your success can be measured consistently, probably accounting for about 85% of your outcome with the Success Formula.

The extra 15% that drives success is the player's belief in themselves to get it done, regardless of circumstances or challenges. Belief builds over time, through consistent steps, like climbing a ladder.

The Belief Ladder represents the steps players progress through as they build belief.

THE BELIEF LADDER

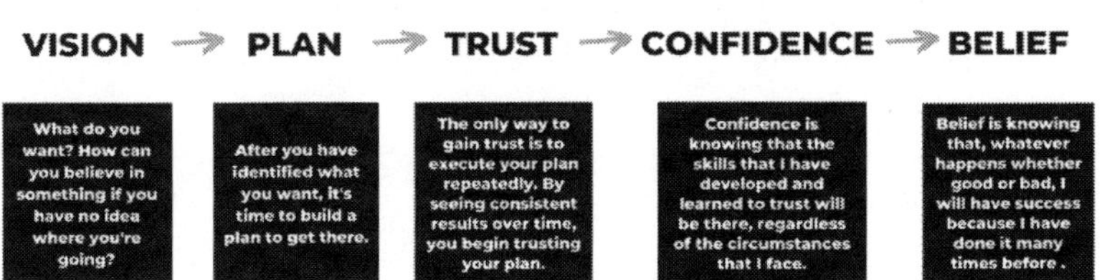

Belief is THE complete knowledge that you can handle anything that comes your way. It requires intense focus on the task at hand and acceptance of the good and bad. It highlights the most critical factor – YOU.

When a player's self-belief is high, they exude it in how they carry themselves, approach challenges, and bounce back after failure. High-belief competitors have an acceptance that no single outcome will define their self-image or derail them from their goals. Therefore, BELIEF is immensely powerful.

But you do not have belief all the time. It waxes and wanes.

When you have high belief, circumstances become more consistent with your vision and intentions, and you tend to see those circumstances with a positive outlook. If you believe it, you begin to see everything confirming it.

You do not get caught up in unrealistic expectations when you are full of belief because the future, where expectations live, is beyond your immediate focus. The only thing that matters is the next challenge because you KNOW you can handle it.

When you lack belief, you put too much value on the results. You must have proof you are on the right path. You need things to go your way. As a result, you do not trust yourself to handle the variable events of the performance.

You build belief through your training, systematically improving your talents and skills, and preparing those skills for the elevated pressure of competition. When you combine a mental game full of belief with adequate skills, you prepare yourself for the randomness and uncertainty of competition.

Belief demonstrates you can manage anything.

Belief is built by KNOWING, not expecting.

It is all about you. That is why it is so powerful yet volatile.

So how do you capture the secret ingredient of the best competitors?

You build it – you build belief.

Belief starts with a clear vision of what you want. If you do not have a clear objective, you will never stay focused on the goal instead of getting distracted by the daily challenges. I want my players to tell me what they want. I do not judge their desires or goals.

If it is in your heart, I want to hear it. I have had players tell me they want to make it to the Major Leagues, and while their coaches had doubts, the players achieved their goal.

If you are willing to declare what you want, then you must be ready to build a plan to achieve it. A plan is where the "rubber meets the road" for athletes, as saying it and doing it separates the best from the rest.

Are you willing to do what it takes to succeed?

There are a variety of plans that you can develop to build belief. I have found that the most effective methods focus on your strengths, what I call foundations, as opposed to trying to improve weaknesses.

When you chase your weaknesses, you risk losing the sharpness of your strengths without a guarantee that your shortcomings will ever come close to them. The plan that created your strengths is rarely the plan to fix your deficiencies. It is two different processes.

Despite years of advice to focus on your shortcomings, your strengths are the window to your confidence and belief.

You should have foundations across each aspect of your game, including your mental game. Your foundations are the consistent aspects of your game that drive your performance, such as specific mechanical drills and processes. It is essential to optimize your mechanics, strategy, and mental game day in and day out. Instead of waiting for each element to suffer and then work on them, you should devote time every day. Be proactive about training your foundations, and they will improve dramatically.

Most competitors ignore their respective strengths, and as a result, their foundations start to crumble. As they start chasing their weaknesses, they assume their strengths will hold up. But they will not hold up. Instead of getting better across the board, you lose trust in your action and process, losing confidence in yourself. It is a lousy death spiral, started by not having a systematic plan to improve your game.

You must continue to work on the mundane, minor details. It is not sexy or sophisticated, but the little things become the big things. Those foundational elements are consistent in your game. If you look back to the times you performed at your best, more than likely, there were two to three consistent drivers that led to your success. Why not train them proactively?

As you build more powerful foundations, you can develop other aspects of your game. But do not get impatient as you build skills. Training elite skills requires time to build trust.

Your plan MUST be written down, planning each day of training and recording your progress. It is like going to the grocery store without a shopping list and coming home with multiple desserts but forgetting why you went in the first place. You will lose discipline and skip the most challenging aspects of training. If you do not have a progress journal, the question is "why not?"

Trust is built through consistent actions producing predictable results and in controlled settings, training, or practice. While it eventually develops in competition, you must start building trust in controlled environments like practice. When you trust your training, you believe your actions will produce the desired results in competition.

Trust is formed through the extra repetitions after practice, alone in front of a mirror working your mechanics, or watching game film. It is rarely ingrained by a coach or outsider telling you what to do. Trust happens when you immerse yourself into your plan and work through the more minor elements.

As trust gets more robust, you begin to see successes in different competitive environments. Success no longer just happens at practice, but now you start gaining confidence to drive those results in-game or other scenarios. Trust morphs into confidence because you believe you can successfully execute in a variety of settings.

"I know I can" becomes "I am ready." Confidence does not demand as much control over your environment because you can apply your skills to anything when confident. You want to be in the game, and you want to compete.

Confidence only builds through training. It is hard to be confident if you do not trust your process or mechanics.

Results do not breed confidence. They help but do not form the confident player. Results can be risky because you would see a great outcome as somewhat unexpected and random if you are struggling. If you were not struggling, you would not celebrate great results, as you would just get back to work.

Even if you were begging for a magical breakthrough performance, the random great outcome would increase pressure to repeat it. If you lack confidence, that is a disaster waiting to happen.

Why?

Because you will feel the need to repeat the results, and the pressure would build to do it again to be perceived as a valid sign of improvement.

Without a proper foundation, positive results are often the result of unexpected success—kind of like hitting the lottery.

When you are confident, you feel belief building. You will challenge yourself in different settings, even if the risks are higher. It does not matter because you simply want a challenge. If you fail when your confidence is high, it is easy to conceptualize the struggle as a building block. When your confidence is low, those same struggles get perceived as reminders as to why you suck.

As confidence grows, you start embracing the total capacity of who you are, believing in your ability to apply yourself in any circumstance. This belief is a super confidence in self, a higher mental focus on what YOU can do, not how you do it. When your belief is strong, you have immense trust in your training and resiliency to fight through challenges.

Belief does not stay high for long periods of time, so many athletes will share that they feel their focus becomes more directed with high belief. It is a powerful feeling to have a complete awareness of your capacity to compete.

When belief gets high, it also gets easier to take shortcuts in your training and lose your discipline. You must train the little things every day. Do not lose discipline because your belief is strong.

The best competitors focus on the most critical aspects of their performance mentality. They eliminate the fluff and ignore the drama.

It is not a secret, is it?

The best competitors are willing to do what it takes.

Are you?

What Are You Willing to Sacrifice?

To perform at your best, you must be willing to make sacrifices. Either you sacrifice your intensity or change the targeted desires of your performance. When you are ready to let go of something important, you open the door for something better to replace it. The problem is that you must be willing to let go of perfection and remove distractions.

You cannot be perfect in every aspect of your life. Striving for success requires vulnerability to any outcome, especially not being perfect. The slight variations in performance must happen, but those differences represent your unique psychological fingerprint. That is where your magic happens.

It is hard to tell professional athletes to show grace to themselves. They are so hard on themselves.

So, I stopped. It does not work. Professional athletes' livelihood depends on their performance, and it is their prerogative to be as hard as they want on their outcomes. The problem is that it comes with collateral damage.

Too often, what competitors say they want does not match their commitment to their craft. Everyone says they want to be the best in the world. Nearly every competitor has told me that their intense desire and work ethic are why they will succeed. Few do the work to overcome the odds.

"Doc, I know what it takes to be the best in the world (or All-American, so insert your goal here). I work hard and will not be satisfied until I achieve it. I will not stop. I will show you."

My reply is easy, "Why are you different than every single person that has come before you? They all say the same thing. What is different about you?"

They stop there.

I have popped their balloon.

For many competitors, success is about saying you want it and then getting angry when falling short. I have learned that if you get mad after falling short, it shows the people in your life that you are better than that or want to succeed. Your reaction is an illusion, however. It is easy to put on the show, get critical of your performance, but forget that you did not make the sacrifices to succeed.

When you want something so intensely, you must believe you can accomplish it. The early successes always give way to struggles, and those struggles become personal, overwhelming, and unrelenting. The early motivations and successes that propelled the initial successes slowly disappear, giving way to newer, more insurmountable obstacles. Those struggles can become so difficult to accept when their simple presence was not expected or anticipated.

Perfectionistic traits become the common coping mechanism to increasing struggles. You believe that the only way to succeed is to improve every aspect of your game to stop the downward slide, but chasing perfection only worsens the difficult challenge.

"But I know I have what it takes!" said every player who has ever sat in my office.

"Do you have what it takes to let go of your perfectionism, to change your definitions of success, and start a different journey? If you cannot shift your definitions, you cannot succeed," is my next discussion point.

Success must be defined in your terms-not your parents, friends, coaches, or any other outsider. Your desires and your feared limitations define your capability to succeed. It is never logical and never based on truth. The radical extremes establish your limits.

You will never achieve at the level you believe you should. That definition of success is unattainable. It is not possible. If your goal is to make the varsity team, your mind will redefine success as a contributor and then be the best on the team. That is normal and completely healthy, but it is not comfortable.

Marie sat in my office one summer afternoon in tears about her prognosis for a potentially career-ending injury. Her once-promising collegiate career was in jeopardy, falling far short of her dreams and expectations. After three years in college, she had only had one season when she was healthy. Even that was a stretch. She had been evaluated by the top surgeons in the country and was given a very low probability of returning to competition.

As she sat in my office, she begged for one more chance to compete. She was willing to endure the pain and suffering to feel the love of competition one more time.

After meeting with her surgeon, he medically cleared her to compete. She was going to postpone her career-ending surgery until after her eligibility was exhausted. It was up to her to determine how to endure the pain. She could not do any additional damage, and she may be able to push through.

She started training again and was having some success in her training sessions. The pain was manageable, and she was so excited to be back in the moment. The first event came and went, and while it was not a success by her previous level of performance, it was a fantastic success by all parties involved. She had her moment again.

Then it all changed.

After two more competitions, she was upset she was not performing at her best. She was improving but not at the rate she wanted. Her definition of success changed with each minor success. Now, she struggled with frustration and disappointment because progress was not there.

I challenged her on her changing the goals.

Her answer was perfect – "Doc, what do you want me to do, just be happy to be competing again? I do this to win!"

Who am I to judge that? I completely get it.

The problem was her frustration was robbing any satisfaction resulting from her successes. By changing the definition of success, she took away the positives and allowed herself to focus on her frustrations. Over time, that will wear anyone out. When all you focus on is a failure, you will begin to think you are failing.

Success requires you to see things differently. I do not want you to accept mediocrity, but every day is a challenge to find the best you have that day.

It may or may not elevate to the level of your ideals, but that is not possible every day. The same factors are not always under your control in every competition.

Your new definition of success must focus on determining what you can create each day. Instead of chasing things that need improvement, you need to spend that time investing in the things you do well, what I think are your superpowers. Stop wasting your time on the negatives.

You do not need to feel confident, feel good, or be mentally tough today to find your best. There are no conditions for pushing forward. Change your definition to the effort you put forward in the moment.

9

IT IS TIME TO TAKE CONTROL

"If you cannot do the little things right, you will never do the big things right."

---Admiral William H. McRaven

Ninth Commander of the United States Special Operations Command (SOCOM)

A client I was meeting with said to me, "Doc, I have been lying to you. I have been listening to our discussions, reading the notes from our sessions, and not doing anything with the information. I do not know why, though.

What is wrong with me?"

"Not a darn thing," I replied.

People do not change unless they are ready. As a clinical psychologist, very few clients come in to make wholesale changes in their lives. Most only make the adjustments in the areas of their lives that have the most pain. Few invest in making changes for the sole purpose of improving.

I asked him, "So if you have the information and deep down, you know what you need to do, what is holding you back?"

"I do not know what to do with the ideas. I mean, I am a pretty good player who has had quite a bit of success out on Tour. I guess I am not sure what to do first," he replied.

My player was not just pretty good – he was a phenomenal player. He was top 50 in the World Rankings and was a multiple-time winner on the PGA Tour. He first sought my services because he was intrigued by the mental side of the game, and he wanted to learn more. There was nothing wrong with his game or life.

He appeared to be scratching an educational itch throughout our sessions as if he was interested and just wanted to learn general concepts. I knew that and would answer his questions with the best answers that I could summons. The conversations were fun, even if they did not result in dramatic changes in thought processes or behavior. I took the approach that he would progress into more comprehensive and personal information when he was ready. I just did not expect him to be so protected, and to be honest, I did not even realize it.

I knew he was a natural skeptic. His antagonistic nature made our conversations more engaging, but they also felt like an academic interrogation. I guess I felt good because I could banter with him on complex topics, but I failed him. Instead of getting to the core of his needs, I allowed myself to be a token in his game.

After our conversation, I took a deep dive into his game and statistics. His performances were mediocre to below average, and I had missed this downward trend. Our conversations were so good and engaging that he had fooled me. He had kept me off the complex, challenging topics.

The phone rang again.

"Doc, let's put it all out on the table. I think the information is helpful, but I am frustrated that I have been paying you and doing nothing with it.

It is like going to the grocery store and buying all the fresh produce, only to go out to eat every night until your groceries spoil.

I have been trying to figure out why I am resisting so much. We may not figure that out in this conversation so give me something to kick start me. I am ready!"

I could not let this slide this time. The fact he was saying, "I am ready!" was encouraging, but I had missed the signs several times in the past. He made me feel important, but I was not doing a good job.

"Why is this time any different?" I asked. "I can give you the tools, the strategies, and the meditations, but if you do not believe in them, you are just going through the motions. I need you to figure out why now."

"Doc, let me be honest. I have not done anything because I was worried that I would spend all this time working on my mental game and not see any positive results. But the other day, I was playing the final round with one of the top players in the world, and I noticed he moved differently, prepared so much better than me, and was so much more organized than me. He kicked my butt but not because his talent was better than mine. He was so much better mentally prepared.

I have been so mediocre this year, leaving every tournament disappointed and frustrated. I feel like I am losing valuable time and opportunities left in my career. The young guys are so much better as rookies than I was. If I do not find a way, I am going to be the player who never reached his potential."

Holy cow!

He just described being stuck in Suckville! But it was more than that. He had admitted that he was scared to implement the new strategies just in case they did not work. He was worried he was running out of time, and as a result, he found himself getting more frustrated with each below-average performance.

"I am now ready. Give me a starting spot," he begged.

I gave him a simple task to do every day – to journal his progress. It was my test to see if he was motivated. More importantly, I needed to know if he was going to keep at it.

I know people do not stick to their intentions. New Year's Resolutions fail without question. New diets do not make it to Friday. And people abandon their gym memberships in February in record numbers.

My dissertation in graduate school examined the factors that prevented patients from taking their diabetes medication. My study group consisted of very low-income patients who could not afford the medicine, so the hospital had created a "free medication program." The doctors in the program needed the patients to take their medications because of the long-term negative health impact of diabetes. If the patients would take the medication, the doctors could prevent many of the complications. It sounded like an excellent program to reduce the adverse effects of a prevalent disease but had significant long-term difficulties.

After two years of the free medication program, there was no increase in medication adherence. In other words, it did not help at all.

Over the years, patients had complained they could not take their medications because it was too expensive. So why did this not improve? That question was the purpose of my dissertation research.

The study required our research team to reach out to patients enrolled in the medication program and inquire about their barriers to treatment. Using an adapted assessment tool and checklist, patients would select those issues from various choices, including some that appeared to be "off-the-wall." On the research side, the assessment targeted different categories of barriers, from the cost of medication to their understanding of the diabetes disease process.

The most reported barrier to treatment was the cost of medication. Despite asking about financial costs in several different ways, those questions related to the costs of the medication and therapy kept being the most common issue to treatment adherence.

But the medication was free. Why did it continue to be the most frequent barrier to treatment?

The cost of the medication was not just a financial issue. There was a significant aspect of it that was psychologically based. When the medication was too financially expensive, it provided patients with an easy excuse not to follow their stringent diabetes protocol. When the medication was easily obtainable, it showed that it was not the financial cost but rather the psychological investment of a healthy lifestyle that was the most difficult.

Either you are all in or all out. How hard is it to take a medication that can improve your life? Not as easy as you think when you must be accountable across several areas of your life. The lack of improvement was insightful for the treatment teams as well. Instead of getting angry with the patients for not taking their medication, the doctors and nurses seemed to show more compassion with the difficulty of a healthy lifestyle.

Sometimes, the issues holding you back are not as big as you make them out to be. In your mind, those barriers may appear massive, but if you can learn to see them from a different perspective, you may just find a way through the difficulties.

Do You Need a Formal Invitation?

My client, the professional golfer, had been dipping his toes in the water for far too long but not fully committing. He got embarrassed by the top-ranked player, and it upset him.

His decision to get started was not an impulsive decision. He evaluated his game and realized he wanted to be better. Doing it required a commitment that he had not allowed to this point.

I had recommended the proper steps forward many times, but it was not the right time for him to fully invest in the mental game for various reasons. Working on the mental game simply meant working through discomfort for far too long, not building a world-class mental framework. No matter how many times we talked about it, how much his swing coach recommended it, or the in-depth conversations with his wife, nothing was going to happen until he permitted himself to move forward.

That permission required him to fully appreciate the positives and the negatives of fully committing to the possibilities of the mental game.

No one is going to make it easier for you. There is no need for that to happen.

To break free from Suckville, you must tap into the resources that you already have, make some slight alterations in your approach or process, and protect yourself from those who may not have your best interests in mind. It is up to you and how bad you want to succeed.

The difference between success and failure is so slight. It is about timing, presence, and showing up. Sometimes, it is a chance encounter with a long-lost friend, a spark of insight, or a "lucky" bounce that changes the course of your future. Those minuscule differences are why it is so hard to predict what drives success. The secret is in the details. If you are caught up in the drama, you will not be prepared for those moments.

You must be ready to embrace success. There is nothing wrong with you, and you are not broken.

The issue is that you have lost faith in yourself. I want you to stop looking for breakthrough moments. Instead, I want you to build your future by the way you think, act, and perform.

You are capable of great things. I want you to compete with indestructible belief again. There is no more incredible feeling than knowing you can face any challenge and endure.

In the next section, I will give you some tangible actions to build your belief and drive success in your game.

10

CHANGE THE RULES OF THE GAME

The longer you stay stuck in Suckville, the harder it gets to find anything positive about your life and game. Struggle works to ignore success, but it attracts failure with such ease that everything gets stacked against you. You must believe you can break free, and you will.

You have been able to overcome struggles many times in the past. There is no reason that you will not only succeed but become better through your growth. All success requires an element of struggle and grind, so do not give in to the drama around you.

Necessary changes will be needed in the way you think, what you do, and the feedback you want. Each will be gradual shifts and nothing dramatic. You are not broken, just doubting your abilities.

Doubt is the emotion that keeps you stuck in Suckville.

Can I succeed?

Can I reach the level of performance that I have romanticized in my head?

Can I do it when it matters the most?

Everyone has doubts. It is core to the human experience, but it is always front and center for the competitor. It shapes your mindset and influences your actions.

Doubt tells you that you are not good enough at the exact moment when you need to hear the encouragement that you are. Doubt highlights your weaknesses and glorifies your mistakes. Doubt tells you that others are much better than you, and it is a waste of time to try.

Doubt creates the foundation for Suckville to begin overtaking your mental game.

As painful as doubt can feel, it is never foreshadowing the future. Learn to see doubt as a reminder of where you want to improve and not a signal you are not good enough. Find the value in doubt instead of the anxiety of it.

It is how you look at it.

To understand doubt and how it impacts you, you must explore its origins.

Doubt starts to emerge as you push towards something out of your comfort zone and requires you to break free from the normal. As you grasp an idea, desire, or goal, doubt looks to protect you against the potential dangers in the vicinity.

Because doubt is an internal process, you often get stuck worrying if you can prosper, succeed, or sustain excellence. It has nothing to do with your circumstances or challenges outside you. It is an inside game and the most challenging of them all.

Confronting doubt forces you to determine how badly you want to succeed. If you do, you will improve your shortcomings, find additional purpose in the competition drama, and narrow your focus.

When doubt intensifies, it can cripple your progress. If you resist the presence of doubt or see it as a threat, it will create an insurmountable wall of why you cannot succeed and why the risks are too high. The more you have doubt, the more you look for short-term fixes and escape from the pain. You do not believe you can withstand the pain.

But you can do it. You have done it before, and you will push through this period of struggle again. It is time to face the doubt, the battle, and the fear head-on.

Change and growth will not happen fast. There will not be a miraculous shift in your performance where the anxiety, frustration, and disappointment suddenly go away. It will take time.

You will have to change your perspective on the game, your journey, and your struggles. Your struggles and shortcomings are not defining moments of your future any more than each bump and pothole are predicting enjoyment for a road trip. Doubts may make the journey less comfortable but do not have to knock you off your trajectory.

You reflect your perspective and attitude. Regardless of how hard it gets, you own the power to shift your perspective and mindset.

You are going to have to change your definitions of success and struggle. They have become warped over the months and years of your competition. Success is not about the views at the top of the mountain but rather the minor victories you create during every level of the climb. Start to see growth through your daily achievements.

It is time to increase your effort level on the right things. You spend far too much time on the drama around your performance and not enough energy to improve your performance level. You must determine what needs your direct attention and invest everything you have in those factors. Let go of the conflicts and distractions that rob your energy. It is not worth your time.

Your negative thoughts will try and take over your experience. When things get challenging, your mind becomes a fertile ground for fear, negativity, and insecurities to grow. Your thoughts will increase in frequency and intensity.

You begin to have overwhelming thoughts questioning your grittiness and resilience. Even though there is always risk in competition, it becomes more potent as drama increases.

"When am I going to have to quit?"

"Who is going to quit on me?"

"Can I do this?"

You are spending too much time thinking about those questions and worrying that the game will defeat you. Quitting is not an option in this pursuit. You would not have come this far to give up when it gets hard. You may not achieve the success you want, and you will never hit your mythical potential, but walking away and letting struggle win cannot be an option.

Finally, it is time to grow your toolbox and learn to trust what you have available to you. You are not missing anything. Your tools need to be sharpened. When in the depths of Suckville, it is easy to see your shortcomings, but it is time to know what you have at your disposal, learn new skills, and learn how to apply them better.

The journey is always unknown. It is never like another's, it never follows the exact steps you have done before, and it is never easy. You are more prepared for the uncertainty of the journey than you believe you are, and you will be able to persevere by merely pushing forward. It comes down to your experience and owning that essence.

You must get proficient at managing the unknown and finding what you can control through it all.

Learn to Sit in It

"Don't be in a hurry to screw up!"

The advice I received during my first month in college stays with me today. For so many things in life, I want to get to the solution so fast that I blast through the things that make me successful. Coach Randy Davis was responsible for leading the younger players on the team, ensuring we got to where we needed to be, and understanding the program's culture.

"I hate freshmen! You guys make my life miserable. Instead of paying attention, you just put your head down and plow into everything like a bull in a China cabinet." That was our introduction to Coach Davis.

He wanted us to pay attention and not be in such a hurry to act. Far too often, players want to do something instead of learn something, and their doing is based on the wrong information. I never forgot that advice, and I made it a part of my approach. I wanted to learn first and do second.

Slow down for a minute, and it will save you years. When your mind slows down, it can identify the path forward. Unfortunately, you have become good at starting and then figuring it out. You do not make it easy.

Your urgency to get out of the pain has caused many more problems than the frustration of staying too long in the misery. I know you want to break free and start having the success you dreamt of, but be patient, purposeful, and productive. You do not have to escape the discomfort of struggle, and you do not have to fear uncertainty. You are prepared to handle anything.

Learn to sit still while the chaos of the world spins around you. Do not be in a hurry, as you will only mess up.

The Foundation of a Successful Mindset

Before getting into the specific actions needed to break free from Suckville, I need to lay out some foundational perspectives that drive success. Each of these provides the necessary support to achieve your goals. If any of your foundational elements is not understood, it can create significant challenges for you.

It is like building a house on a rickety foundation. Everything you build on that foundation will be vulnerable because of the weak grounding. The weight of the structure will cause a complete collapse. But if the structure was built on a strong foundation, the entire house can sustain the weight.

Your struggle is not long-term unless your mental foundations are weak.

1. Life Is Not Fair

It amazes me how chronically ill children in the hospital have the best outlook on life despite their conditions. Why are those with the most to lose able to find the silver lining in every storm cloud?

Why are those with the greatest tragedy in their past the most motivated to create a better future?

Does it seem those who have the bleakest futures can do what so many of us struggle to do? To accept their circumstances and start building out a new future.

Life is not fair. Some people deserve better, and some should not have the pleasure of what they have.

It is easier to complain about your bad breaks, the injustices you had to experience, and how nothing goes your way instead of making the most of your opportunities. No one cares about your bad luck. If life were fair, you would not live it.

"Someone else has had better breaks in life."

"A colleague got the benefit of the doubt and got promoted."

"Another business got a big contract."

"A teammate gets all the media attention."

It is always something.

Yet, the young child sitting in the hospital with tubes, leads, and medical charts the size of encyclopedias can see the opportunities in his/her life. At the same time, we magnify minor struggles into immense burdens.

What is up with that? Why is that the case?

Life is not fair, life was never fair, and life will never be fair. Life is life, and that is all that it is.

Some people have better opportunities, and some have brutal conditions in their lives. Some players seem to get the best breaks, and others must overcome every possible setback simply to keep playing. It is not fair and never will be. Life does not keep score.

You must accept that life is not living you; you must live the life you have and make the most of it.

It is impossible to determine fairness. It is all about your perspective and what you fear you are missing. Your insecurity will determine the boundaries of humanity.

When you learn to accept that fairness is impossible to achieve, the playing field becomes level. Accepting that life is not fair empowers you to make the most of what you do have. When you stop fighting against your circumstances, you start pushing through the struggles. When you stop comparing yourself to others, you begin to see how amazing you really are.

Life is complex and requires all that you have to navigate the ups and downs. Getting caught up in what you do not have compared to others will only steal your power from persevering.

Your circumstances are nothing but growth steps, challenges to define who you are. Too many get caught up comparing their conditions with those around them, only to feel more powerless because it is not fair. Remember, life is hard, and it is undoubtedly not equitable. It will break you down if you give in to the injustice of life. It is your responsibility to make something of your life.

2. Integrity Does Not Lead to Success

I was taught that good fortune results from hard work, relentless efforts, and treating people equally. But I also understood that it was not and never will be absolute. The formula for success is never a perfect solution.

Unfortunately, neither the game nor society adequately delivers justice. While integrity should be the standard, the truth is that integrity is not a guarantee for justice.

Sometimes good things happen to bad people, and bad things happen to good people. The formula is never perfect.

It is hard to do the work, make the sacrifices, and lay it all on the line and come up short. To make matters worse, to see another who did not give all that you did, did not make the sacrifices, or chose a more straightforward pathway to succeed only pours salt in your wounds. But that is not your responsibility or burden. That is theirs. It may catch up to them, and it may not.

I do not care what round you got drafted.

I do not care how many accolades you had in the past.

I do not care how many awards you have received from professional organizations.

I do not care how many hours you studied for the exam.

I do not care how many jobs you passed over to come work with me.

I do not care that you could have been something if things were better in your favor.

What I care about is how you will take on the next challenge and opportunity. That is what I care about, and that should be your attention.

I have experiences in my past that were wonderful. I grew up in a fantastic family. I was blessed to be a part of and contribute to the best baseball program in the country. I currently work with the elite of the elite competitors and consult with the country's top athletic department. I have a fantastic wife and two beautiful daughters that are driving success in their own way.

I am fortunate to be where I am today. I have made sacrifices and decisions that many have disagreed with. I have listened to consultants tell me how it should be only to regret not listening to my instincts. I have caused strife with some mentors who felt that my professional pursuits were inconsistent with their vision for my career because I was "selling out my degree." I left a very lucrative and stable job to start my own business in one of the most volatile economic periods of our lifetime. I did so without any college savings for my high school daughters.

What did I have?

I had determination, fueled by a work ethic established by my parents from an early age. I had a competitive mindset from my childhood that was a part of every conversation in my household from the earliest memories that I have. I had tremendous support from my wife (and business partner), children, and parents.

Others have succeeded faster than me. I have seen their successes, and it has created overwhelming anxieties and disappointment in me. I know of some who have taken avenues that I morally, ethically, and personally disagree with. Even if I could do what they did, I still would not.

When I learn of their work's praise and admiration at the national level, I still grimace today. But that is not my responsibility. I have to work harder, give more, and drive my determination to the next level. And never assume success is coming.

Being a high-quality human does not guarantee success. Being a low integrity person does not guarantee miserable performances. So why does it matter?

Success does not necessarily come from the type of person you are. Integrity should never be valued based on your accomplishments.

The people in the lead may have impeded others' progress to succeed, or maybe they had to make self-centered decisions at the expense of others and shortcuts to get ahead. If their primary goal was to succeed, then they did that. Their success does not mean they did it the correct way.

Critics of athletes and teams have long struggled with this foundation. It is fodder for social media.

"Team A cheats at recruiting…." but insert your rival as Team A.

The New England Patriots have been accused many times and found guilty of skirting various rules. Still, year in and year out, their level of play far outperforms the possible gains from the organization's indiscretions.

The Houston Astros and Boston Red Sox have been implicated in a significant cheating scandal most recently. Major League Baseball has implicated them in a scheme of tipping pitches to their hitters. Using alleged buzzers and closed-circuit televisions, they supposedly used the system to put themselves in a position to win the World Series in 2017 and 2018, respectively. But the Patriots', Red Sox, or Astros' championships have never been vacated.

It seems that the easiest thing to do when losing is to attribute another's success to how they maximize the grey area in the rule book or highlight minor infractions as reasons for their success. While I hate cheating in any form or fashion, it is not uncommon for the top performers to look for ways to gain an advantage over their competition, even if that motivation results in breaking the rules.

There is a fine line between playing by the rules and breaking the rules. As you get closer to the line, it becomes effortless to cross that line, even if unintentional at that time. I have had the chance to spend some time with those who have crossed the line. I want to know the psychological motivation at that moment. With almost uniformity, they say it was a series of events that got out of hand. Their original intention was to find an angle, a rule-abiding way, but one decision led to an action that led to another choice. Eventually, they realized they were way across the line and too far away.

Do you remember an Olympics without a doping scandal? What about the Tour de France?

Every sport has had periods of embarrassment due to the actions of its members. Every business sector in the world has had its problems too. From the energy sectors to religious organizations have defining moments considered black eyes by its constituents.

Obsessing about the integrity of your competitors can destroy your positive energy. You must own your integrity. Your reputation will always outlive your accomplishments. Competitors who choose to trade their integrity for victories will have to deal with the consequences at some point. That is their issue, not yours.

3. Your Response Determines Your Future

You can never protect bad things from happening to you. Success and failure follow the odds and probabilities of life. You will go into slumps, you will get yelled at by your coaches and managers (if they are good leaders), and you will doubt yourself.

Great coaches are going to demand a lot from you. Many times, it may seem to be harsh. But your responsibility is to determine your response, not get caught up in the drama of their message. Your response is everything.

You have gone too long trying to prevent adverse outcomes from happening. If you are willing to compete, you have to be prepared to manage the struggle as much as the glory. You cannot have one without the other.

You are not prepared for the struggle because of the way you have been approaching your competition. You have dreamt about success and visualized the great performances, only to be disappointed when reality hits. As a result, the mere appearance of struggle sets you off emotionally. You have not been able to handle it, and with every battle, it gets harder and harder to deal with it. It has consumed you.

Imagine walking out of your house in the morning into the pouring rain and freezing temperatures outside. The sky is dark, threatening, and ominous. The wind is blowing, the trees are shaking, and puddles of water have pooled up on your walkway. You know it is raining hard and only going to get worse.

How do you react?

What if your hands are full, you are carrying your coffee, backpack, and car keys?

The more demands you have, the less likely you can respond rationally and effectively. Your ability to mentally maneuver the struggle will be compromised. Your emotions will heighten, your frustration worsens, and you will make more mistakes in getting in your car.

Will you stop, yell at the sky, and think the whole day is ruined?

I hope not!

I would hope you would put some of the stuff in your hands down, slow down, and not be in a hurry to make it worse.

When you are overwhelmed, you REACT. The more mentally flexible you are, the more likely you will RESPOND to the challenge.

The most crucial factor that you own is how you respond to life challenges. Dr. Viktor Frankl, a psychiatrist and author of *Man's Search for Meaning*, suggests that while many unpredictable and uncomfortable things can happen to you, what matters is how you learn to control how you respond.

Frankl was a prisoner in the inhumane concentration camps of the Nazi German regime and observed a fascinating phenomenon of his fellow prisoners as they struggled with the atrocities of the camps. Those who could find any purpose for their struggle seemed to have the mental ability to persevere, and those who could not quickly lost their will to live.

A purpose had to be challenging to find in those conditions. Those who could identify a lesson hidden in the mystery of their inhumane treatment gained a perspective that empowered them to sustain their existence. It appeared that those who lost their will to live could not find any purpose for suffering. The last of "human freedoms" was one's ability to choose his/her attitude, observed Frankl.

You always own that choice.

Psychologist Dr. Edith Egars was also an Auschwitz survivor as a young teenager. In her memoir, *The Choice*, she vividly described the challenging, painful moments in her life and the effect they had on her for the rest of her life. For far too long, she allowed her experiences to destroy her attitude, making it hard to have healthy relationships and a productive life. Even though she could not change the past, she could see the past from a different perspective.

For too long, the horrors while in Auschwitz continued to inflict damage on her, as if her captures were continuing to torture her. To stop the torture, she had to make a bold decision to change something. Her perspective had to change. Because she decided to reframe her past, she gained more emotional power over the painful memories of the past.

How?

Is it even possible to mute the past?

Yes, by how to decide to face life. Do you react or respond?

There is a distinct difference between reacting and responding to life. They are not the same. In this difference lies the secret to your future.

When you react to a stressful situation or a threat, the primary motivation driving your thoughts and behaviors is your intense desire to avoid the pain and negative consequences. Your drive is not to work through it but to escape any negative experiences because of it. You are trying to survive the stress. If given a choice to avoid it altogether, you will run from it. The goals are avoidance and self-preservation.

You do not face the threats with a logical perspective. There is no time for that. You think and move so fast because the threat is coming too quickly. Time goes fast, and decisions are muddled.

I call those that react, Reactors.

On the other hand, there are Responders.

Responders face the same challenges, but the primary emotional drive is to work through the problem instead of avoiding the pain. Responders know it will be hard, likely painful, and a long process, but the challenge is not bigger than them. Pain is not to be avoided but used to become better for future challenges.

For Responders, their decision-making motivation is about facing the challenge head-on, finding a solution, and getting better because of the experience. There is no intention to avoid but instead to work through the challenges. Responders rarely blame, while Reactors get consumed with who is to blame and why the struggle appeared in the first place.

In a competitive environment, Responders differ significantly from Reactors. In the heat of the moment, Responders can accept the racing thoughts, the increased arousal, and the flood of emotions but learn to find the purpose now. Reactors do not want to make mistakes, but Responders give their total effort and accept that mistakes may happen.

That is the primary difference in every setting – the fear of mistakes. You cannot prevent 100% of errors from happening, but you must learn to respond to them with all your effort and mental strength. You have survived, and you will sustain more if you know to Respond and not React.

4. Trust Carefully

When stuck in Suckville, it is easy to trust the wrong person, those who may not have your best interests in mind or do not have the skills or experience to help you. You must protect yourself at all costs. It does not mean to be emotionally unavailable, but rather be careful who you allow into your life.

When you are struggling, it is easy to seek answers from anyone willing to give them to you. People by nature do want to help, but that does not mean their information is helpful to you.

Every piece of information you seek becomes like an addict scoring their next hit. You must have the solution, the next quick fix, and the immediate reassurance RIGHT NOW!

Trust is such a tricky psychological concept. When you have it, you know it. When you do not, you are hurt from the lack of it. There is no place in between.

In your life, there are guides and distractions. Knowing how to differentiate between the two can make or break your performance future. Authentic guides do not insert themselves for their gain as they are catalysts for your growth.

Authentic guides lead with perspective and wisdom. They know the journey because they have been on it themselves, never influencing for their gain. They do not try and sell you on their greatness.

An authentic guide walks step-by-step with you, even if they are not physically there with you, providing little nudges so you can find your way through the chaos of competition. Their knowledge is more profound than the circumstance. Trust is never the issue for a guide because they are not trying to gain your trust.

> That probably sounds conflicting.
>
> An authentic guide does not search for your trust. A proper guide already has it.
>
> An authentic guide exudes trust and faith in the process through their interaction, whether direct or hands-off. There are no quick fixes, and they know that you will struggle as you emerge. They do not react; they respond to your struggles and support you fully.
>
> I have struggled with this so much in my life, so I speak from experience. I have always stumbled to trust myself in my business and competitions. It seemed that I was still jumping between the shiniest advice and the quickest promises to change my circumstances. If there was a gadget, a consultant, or a guru, I was all-in. I would try and convince everyone else of their value instead of learning to build up my confidence.
>
> In the end, I was always disappointed. Nothing ever seemed to work because I tried to trust the wrong people, probably because I was looking for the shortcuts to success. I should have known that quick fixes are nothing more than false promises leveraged on my hope.

You did not end up here overnight. There is a path forward, and there is a process to develop to help you get there.

You must learn to trust yourself. You can persevere and have success. When you realize that your circumstances no longer own you and your attitude can rise above the challenges, you create emotional freedom. I know it is not easy, and there are times that your circumstances seem unrelenting, but you must see what you can do despite your conditions.

If I bet against you, would you get motivated to find a way through the challenges?

If your circumstances were to improve suddenly, would it be easier to get motivated? Would anything change other than the path in front of you?

Probably not. You cannot determine your ability by anything around you. You own the right to your future regardless of your past.

11

CHANGE YOUR PERSPECTIVE

A teacher stood in front of her 5th-grade classroom and showed a picture to her students. It was a black and white framed portrait of a middle-aged man. His face was weathered, with dark wrinkles around his eyes and a worn expression, reflecting years of hard, stressful work. His skin was rough as leather, and it was dirty, smeared with grime and grease. He wore a torn jacket, and he looked unkempt overall.

The teacher asked the kids what they saw. The students described the picture in detail, focusing on the individual elements of his profile with great attention. Then, one boy in the back said, "he looks homeless." That opened the discussion. After that, every single point highlighted this "homeless" man's pain and suffering, making judgments of his plight as a homeless man in their community. The adjectives used to describe the man became more and more cynical with each comment.

"How do you know he is homeless?" the teacher asked.

"Look at him; he is so dirty," one young girl replied. "He hasn't showered, and he probably smells."

As the class laughed, the teacher asked a follow-up question, "Is there any other way to look at him? Could it be that he was cleaning up his house? Cleaning his fireplace? Or even building a fort for his grandchildren?"

"Let me tell you what I see," the teacher added.

"This is my dad. He owns a large construction company and likes to work hands-on with his teams. When he was 14 years old, his father died in a tragic accident, so he started working on construction crews to support the family. He believes that a hard day's work ends with you being exhausted, dirty, and everything on your "to-do" list checked off. He has provided for my family his entire life and does not like taking vacations. He loves to work.

I don't see tired, dirty, or homeless. I see the opposite. I see a provider, a father, and a whole, loving heart."

At that moment, the door to the classroom opened, and her father walked in.

Gone were the filthy, disheveled work clothes, replaced by the crisply ironed shirt and pants like he was going to church. He had a perfectly groomed face, and it radiated with a beaming smile.

She asked the students, "Now, what do you see?"

They saw a father-a very proud father.

What You Perceive May Make You Anxious

Those 5th-graders are not much different than you when you analyze your performances. You make a ton of assumptions, and very few of them are based on factual data. It is easier to make an emotional conclusion than look at reality.

How many judgments do you make with only part of the story?

How often do you look right through your reality to latch onto the negatives swirling around you?

With every experience you have, you choose to see those experiences, either as positive or negative, as an opportunity or a threat. Your mental framework and attitude follow the lead of your judgments and assumptions.

What you perceive is neutral; you just add the seasoning, drama, and interpretation to create your attitude.

You are not always in total control of how you interpret your circumstances. When the slightest sense of threat is identified, even subconsciously, your mind builds energy (e.g., arousal, anxiety) to get ready to meet that threat. The increased arousal happens outside your conscious awareness as all you feel is your built-up energy.

Assume I take you to a national forest and tell you that you have five hours to hike five miles to reach the cabin in the woods. I will even give you a map to make it easier.

How would you feel?

Excited?

Nervous?

Uncertain?

If it is a competition, you might feel excited and want to get the journey started to gain a head start on your opponents.

Would other factors contribute to how you feel? Would the time-of-day matter?

If you are leaving at 8 am, your level of arousal will probably be more excited than stressed. The prospects of navigating the challenges of the forest only get you more prepared for the uncertainty of the journey.

If you are going at 8 pm in the pitch darkness of the forest, you will likely feel different, probably a bit more anxious than leaving in the morning. You will be hypervigilant to every noise, believing that a nocturnal animal has you in its sights for dinner. You may be more careful with each step you take, cautious not to lose your footing and fall into the dark caverns of the mysterious woods.

It is the same path and the same journey, but the time of day changed your perception of threat. You simply interpreted things differently.

Imagine if there had been a series of vicious bear attacks on that path in the past week. What does that do to your attitude, arousal level, and overall mindset?

I believe your arousal level may approach the intensity of panic attacks, and you would look for any way out of the challenge. It would be hard to venture into the darkness of the forest knowing the threats waiting for you.

Now, what if you were a trained bear hunter?

Probably different altogether!

You often let your emotions drive the judgments of your performances, too. If you feel you are improving, you will see improvements. But if you think you are struggling, you will only see areas that are not performing up to your expectations. The difference is the lens of how you see things, and you create that lens!

Many factors contribute to your overall perspective. It is not a born-in trait, nor is it entirely determined for the rest of your life. Every experience creates the essence of where you are today, and that shifts the lens by which you see the world.

Your perspective is 100% unique to you. There is no way to get someone to see the world the way you do. Your perspective is a lens that determines what you see and influences your underlying psychological beliefs and core values. With each experience, that lens becomes formed into a powerful window. As a result, your perspective influences your attitude.

You create your attitude, experiences, and confidence in how you see the world. These factors enhance your readiness and openness to take on an uncertain future. Your perspective is your lens to view the entirety of the world. Sometimes, you can zoom in and, other times, see the entire landscape. If you fear struggle, you will only see pain, misery, and darkness. If you see hope, you will see the light illuminating the openings to walk through.

It is all about how you see things. You ultimately choose that.

Your walk into the uncertainty of the woods is a perfect illustration of how performance arousal/anxiety builds and causes problems. When there is uncertainty over your safety and the potential outcomes, it alters your perspective, hijacks your flexibility to see anything but danger.

The culprit is uncertainty.

Uncertainty is a powerful trigger for your mind. When you cannot fully determine how much threat is around you, your mind fills in the gaps. The issue is that your mind cannot assume safety, and it fills the void with potential risks. Random noises are no longer neutral but may signal trouble. The increased difficulty to learn a new mechanical skill in your sport becomes evidence of you losing your starting job. Even the smallest margin can create the most significant threat.

If you had absolute certainty about the presence of a threat, your focus would change. Negative thoughts would no longer flood your consciousness, and your mind would shift to purpose, fueled by adrenaline and a tunnel vision. When a threat is identified, the mind prepares the body to fight.

Unfortunately, a clear danger with absolute certainty is rare in performance settings and daily life. Even in the presence of identified risk, uncertainty and ambiguity prevail.

Anxiety fills the gaps in the grey area, shifting your perspective into overtime. Your anxiety leads to constant worry, obsessing about the factors that have no solutions. Worry makes you think you are doing something when you are just digging a deeper hole, but worry rarely has a resolution or end in sight, which builds more fear, anger, and frustration. It is a tough cycle, but one that players in Suckville know all too well.

You must realize that uncertainty will always be present. Instead of seeing it as threatening, learn to see yourself ready for the unknown. It is about you, not the challenge.

Can you be mentally prepared to face the difficulty? Absolutely, but only when you prepare the mind for the challenge.

What is the worst thing that can happen? Probably something you can work through.

You determine your attitude by your perception of the world around you. If you think you can succeed, your attitude will be constructive and positive. On the other hand, if you lack belief in yourself, your attitude will reflect that negativity. It is about the lens through which you see the world.

Everyone has bad days and moments when their attitude is trash. It happens. But you can always become aware of your thoughts, feelings, and attitude.

You do not need a positive attitude to succeed. But it helps.

You do not need to be mentally locked in to compete at your best. But it helps.

You do not need to be excited to be in the competitive arena to give your best effort. But it helps.

Your attitude holds everything together when things get complicated. You do not need a positive attitude to be great, but a negative attitude will make it more difficult for you to succeed.

There will always be factors beyond your control. You must learn what you can control and what is out of your control. Chasing aspects of your performance that are out of your control will make you lose faith in yourself, worsening your attitude. Those factors are how others play, your coach's decisions, and the bad calls of referees.

If you think that all the bad things happen to you, either because of bad luck or because you believe you suck, your attitude will be negatively impacted.

Be the BURN

You must learn to change your perspective by first learning to be aware of what you are thinking and how you can change it. Changing your mindset involves understanding how thought and mental processes form your lens that shape your experiences and attitude.

There is a four-step approach that provides the framework to shift your perspective. It is the BURN strategy. It is as follows:

B – Be aware

U – Understand your negative thoughts

R – Replace thoughts with more flexible, constructive processes

N – Never give in to the moment

Let me take you through each one:

1. Be Aware:

Awareness is critical to success in sports and life. There are so many things going on around you at any given moment, and awareness allows you to slow the chaos to identify what is essential.

Your mind can function at speeds far faster than you can fathom. Because of the mind's speed and heightened awareness when arousal is high, it gets consumed with threats, distractions, and even irrelevant activities.

In the heat of competition, your mind gets consumed with so many factors that it can get overwhelmed. It must manage your internal feelings, external demands, the fans in the stands, and even those pesky random thoughts that pop into your head.

When you are struggling, your mind ramps up your internal intensity to meet every potential demand it faces. Awareness is the mechanism that identifies the threat, risk, or even opportunities at an introductory level. The problem is two-fold: one, you do not slow down enough to even be aware of what is happening, and two, the intensity of the moment makes you judgmental of your mental experiences.

Heightened awareness is the equivalent of standing on the edge of the interstate during rush hour traffic and trying to focus on one car at a time. You become overwhelmed and overstimulated by the sheer speed of each vehicle, not to mention the dangers of standing on the side of a busy highway.

Your mind must determine where to direct its focus based on the mind's level of awareness. While standing on the side of the freeway, you will struggle to focus on just one car unless something grabs your attention.

Awareness involves accepting all that is happening around you, inside you, and to you, but slowing down your focus to listen, observe, and accept without judgment each experience. It is not wrong to simply admit that things are challenging, as awareness allows you to accept the presence of the experience.

Awareness requires you to accept uncertainty as it is, without any judgment. The fact that it is hard is a fact. There is no further drama needed. Facts are not usually up for debate. Being aware of those facts gives you the power to direct your attention as necessary.

You will never have control over everything coming your way, so just be aware of that. The more you resist and the more frustrated you become by the bombardment of challenge, the more power you give to the uncertainty and clutter.

Awareness is a skill that you must learn through experience. It is never easy. Techniques like mindfulness or transcendental meditation, boxed breathing, or exercises like yoga can have tremendous benefits in guiding your awareness.

I use each morning at my desk for my meditation experience. I slowly enjoy a cup of coffee, allowing myself to become fully immersed in the drink. With so many different demands right in front of me, I work to sit and be present with them. I try to transform any morning anxiety into excitement and motivation. As much as I want to do something, the better I get at being present at my desk and enhancing my acceptance of my anxiety slows me down and allows me to focus.

Start practicing awareness at home, in a quiet spot, and pay attention to your thoughts. Do not judge them. Allow them to come and go. Listen to the various random sounds that you hear in the background. Allow your attention to shift towards those sounds and different distractions, and then redirect back to your present experience.

2. Understand Your Negative Thoughts

Thought is the mechanism of your mind to direct your awareness to internal and external demands. Fueled by your perception, both your inner feels and your external triggers, the mind triggers thought to refocus its attention to prepare for action.

Thought is a constant running dialogue in your mind and drives your conscious attention when those thoughts increase your arousal level. Arousal can be increased by good and bad, leading to either excitement or anxiety. Most of the thoughts that grab your attention are negative thoughts. Because negative thoughts highlight the presence of an impending threat, and they will continue to increase in frequency and intensity until it takes over your attention.

Think of negative thoughts like the soundtrack in horror films. If you were to watch many of the iconic horror movies of the last 50 years, like *The Silence of the Lambs*, *IT*, *Psycho*, or *The Shining*, directors would pair tense visual elements with powerful, stress-building, anxiety-provoking music. By incorporating the intensity of the musical aspects, directors are priming you to have an intense reaction to the scene.

Now, if the horror scene has an element of truth, like a mass murderer or stalker instead of an alien attacking from another planet, your arousal level will get cranked up. Even the most minor elements of truth will intensify the experience, especially if that truth has been experienced before. Reality has some truth even in the most feared scenarios, and that is what causes your negative thoughts to grab your attention.

The mind cannot take the risk of ignoring an actual threat, even a low percentage one. So, it elevates the negative thought to your conscious awareness. Your mind makes you pay attention to negative thoughts. When a specific negative thought increases your arousal level, the threat detection of the mind worked.

I do not want you to think your negative thoughts are not real. They are, but they are probably not entirely true or even accurate. But in the slightest chance your negative thoughts may be true, the mind must pay attention.

Negative thoughts always increase as the competition gets more complicated. You will never have positive thoughts in the heat of the moment. If you did, you would ignore them because they are "normal."

When you get upset, worried, or try to suppress negative thoughts, you direct more of your attention to those unproductive thoughts. You raise your arousal level, recruiting more and more negative thoughts. Each negative thought that hijacks your attention brings three to four more additional, more intense negative thoughts with it.

You must understand your negative thoughts and why they occur. By paying attention to your thoughts but not directing additional energy towards them, you regain your power to focus on the task at hand. With greater experience dealing with the intensity of highly competitive moments, you gain wisdom over your thought processes. Once you gain wisdom, you not only understand the negative thoughts, but you know how to perform at your best despite them.

3. Replace with Mental Flexibility

Since mental flexibility is a critical variable in my Success Formula, it requires additional discussion here. I cannot stress the importance of a mental framework built to adapt and adjust to life's successes and struggles. The most successful competitors are determined, motivated, and flexible. You may not see the flexible aspect. They may be so determined that all you see is that extreme side of performance, but they are exceptional at taking any information, opportunity, and challenge and finding their way through it.

Mental flexibility is the main difference I have found between those who succeed at the highest levels and the "wanna-be's." It does not matter what they feel; they can refocus on the task at hand.

Mental flexibility comes in all shapes and sizes. It is not a trait you were born with, but rather, it is something you learn through experience. Over time, you get better and better at flowing with the ups and downs and not getting derailed by a bad outcome, negative thought, or unfortunate turn of events.

You cannot control every aspect of your competitive environment. There are so many factors out of your direct influence. When you get rigid or stubborn in your thinking, you try to fit a square peg in a round hole. The harder you push against the resistance of the struggle, the more mental energy you expend.

Unfortunately, resistance is the standard, and adversity is the norm. I do not believe that great performances will necessarily lead to more accessible experiences. Every new challenge gets increasingly more difficult. You may gain perspective, confidence, and wisdom, but the newness makes it more challenging.

When you get flooded with negative thoughts in the face of

resistance and adversity, you must learn to be flexible and adapt to something more productive. Competition will always tax your mental resources, so having the skills to shift towards effective processes gives you a higher chance of success than getting paralyzed by anger and frustration.

Dr. Steven C Hayes is a psychologist, and author of bestsellers *Get Out of Your Head and Into Your Life* and *The Liberated Mind.* He pioneered a novel form of psychological therapy called Acceptance and Commitment Therapy (ACT), which combines traditional cognitive-behavior therapy with infusions of Buddhism, mindfulness, and stoicism to create the framework for healthy success. ACT has been studied in just about every health and psychological experience and demonstrated robust research support. It is not an idea; ACT is a foundational thought process.

The core elements of ACT involve understanding what is happening to you, and instead of resisting, you shift your perspective to a more effective alternative. By being present with the events around you, you become more engaged and active in implementing healthy behaviors to build your success. ACT empowers you to embrace your mental flexibility and see alternatives instead of barriers.

As a foundational element of ACT, mental flexibility is a significant catalyst for your success. Being mentally flexible is seeing beyond the moment's chaos, realizing what is happening is not personal, and pivoting your mind to something more productive. You can actively shift to an emotion, decision, behavior, or attitude.

When you lack mental flexibility, you can get consumed by a negative emotion, an adverse circumstance, or a bad outcome and cannot let it go. Those negative experiences build on themselves because you cannot redirect your attention. Being flexible is rising above the mental chaos and shifting to something more significant.

Let us look at a few everyday struggles for athletes and how mental flexibility could be productive.

Imagine if you got a bad call from an umpire. There is no doubt that a bad call would upset you. Many athletes would get upset, and most would let that frustration destroy their next few plays. Instead of getting stuck on the frustration, a mentally flexible athlete would move on to the next play, even though they got angry.

Unlike athletes who struggle with their emotions, the mentally flexible athlete would be aware of the negative emotions and be prepared to shift their increased energy into the next challenge. The inflexible athlete would continue arguing and look for validation from their coaches or teammates about how bad the call was for them.

Another example that is prevalent in sports involves playing time. A mentally inflexible athlete would see their lack of playing time as a sign their coach does not believe in them and never like them. One piece of information leads to a cascade of emotions, resulting in negative attitudes, poor play, and bad outcomes. A mentally flexible athlete may get upset about not playing but will pivot their anger into determination to train harder and with greater purpose.

When you get stuck in Suckville, you have bought into the terrible outcomes associated with your struggles, and it is causing you to focus more on the negative events around you. You have lost your mental flexibility. With each perceived conflict, you build more and more "All or Nothing, 100% win or 100% lose" mindsets.

As pressure builds, your mind must expend significant energy to do the simplest tasks. While many of the primary functions are overlearned through repetition, new demands and risky consequences capture your attention.

Being mentally flexible challenges you to understand how increased pressure impacts your thinking. The volume of your thoughts will increase due to the increased mental activity. The overwhelming majority of thoughts will never rise to your conscious awareness, but your cognitive processes perceive the thoughts, assess the environment around them, and keep you successful. Thoughts are just activity, but what they lead to is where you must be mentally flexible.

4. Never Give in to the Moment

Learning to change your perspective must include the understanding that no moment will ever be too big for you. Do not give in to it.

You may lose, get defeated, or struggle, but the moment is never too big for you. You will eventually solve it, but it may not be on your schedule.

Your struggle is not personal and does not mean more difficulties are coming.

Several years ago, I worked with a struggling collegiate athlete who was causing problems for his entire team. He was having a significant challenge in the classroom, and it was impacting his team. His poor performances resulted in more work for the team.

As I showed up for a team meeting, I could feel a distinct tension in the room. The team was seated together in one row, and the offending player sat all by himself in the top row. I asked the group what was going on, and they said they had to run at 5 am because one player had continued to miss class. The team was not happy with my man.

As their voices rose, my player at the center of the storm turned around and yelled at the team. When I got his attention, I asked him why he was so upset when his behavior caused the problem in the first place.

He replied, "I told Coach not to put me in a math class this semester. I always suck at math and did not want to deal with it during the season. I am not going to that class anymore. It is a waste of time."

"So, you chose not to go to class?" I asked.

"Why does it matter? I am going to fail the class anyway. I suck at math. I always have," he shot back.

Suddenly, another member of the team realized what was causing the problem in the room. My player doubted his mathematical abilities, and he was always embarrassed by his struggles in class. It was personal for my player as if he carried a sign around his neck that said "DUMB."

His teammate had figured this out and asked, "if you do not go to class, you don't know if you can be good at it."

A great reply.

After a few minutes of minor academic debate, the player at the center of the conflict agreed to go to class so he could, in his words, "prove all you wrong."

The following week, I showed up for the team meeting, and this player was sitting in the front row. He was smiling ear to ear. He proudly reported that he had made an "A" on his test. It was the first math test in which he had ever made an "A." The team was so excited for him.

He had made struggle personal. Math was hard for him because he struggled to understand the concepts, but he was not stupid or incapable of learning. He had an older brother who was a computer engineer from one of the country's top engineering schools and another with a math degree. Because he always excelled in sports, he just ignored school, despite being intelligent. He had developed a personal reason for his struggles – that he was a "dumb jock."

> No one in his family had called him that, so I wonder why that was so ingrained in him.
>
> If I had to guess, it was his powerful defense mechanism every time he struggled with school. Instead of finding a way to work through it, he gave in to the moment by making it personal.
>
> The moment is not bigger than you. You are more significant than the moment. It just needs your flexible mindset and focused attention to work through it.

Your perspective is everything. It determines how you see challenges and optimizes your mental capacity to face the challenges in your life. Constructive mindsets see opportunities, but negative perspectives see increased struggles. What must change is your perspective. It may be difficult, and you may feel so far away from the success you desire, but you need to learn how to shift your perspective towards your positive traits and the opportunities in front of you. There is light shining on every path before you, but only if you choose to see it.

12

CHANGE YOUR ENVIRONMENT

Suckville is not a destination that has a unique zip code. You are not the first to struggle with something you love and certainly will not be the last. Competitive success requires your psychological vulnerability to be fully open to the good and the bad. If you cannot be vulnerable, then you have a minimal chance of having sustained success.

I received a call from a young baseball player projected to be a first-round draft pick in the upcoming Major League draft. When he spoke, he sounded broken down and exhausted. The game had become foreign to him, and it seemed every day was a test to prove his worth to those around him – scouts, recruiters, media, and teammates.

This young man was special. He had every tool to succeed at the game, but he began to dread games. As a result, his performance was slipping, and the chatter started to increase that he may not have the mental game to be a high-round draft pick. The process was crushing him.

He was fully immersed in Suckville, feeling the burden of the responsibilities of the game. He loved the game, or so he said. In our conversations, he would reflect on his early high school experiences when he was one of the youngest players on the team. The older players mentored him, and he just had to play the game. There was no drama or stress.

The draft projections were accurate and well-deserved. As he started to struggle, the critics began to surface and become more vocal. Opposing players would talk trash about his struggles, focusing on the fact that he struggled against high school talent. Members of the media continued to publish articles and comment on social media, documenting his "fall from excellence." His teammates started to get frustrated with the drama and resented the attention he was receiving.

As a high school senior, he just wanted to enjoy the baseball season and participate in regular high school activities. One of his most significant stressors was the influence of people around him. He felt that some were rooting for him, but significantly more outsiders were reveling in his struggle. The problem was he could not determine who was who.

Some of his detractors would be open about their frustration or doubts, while others would talk behind his back. The tension was noticeable, and he never wanted to be a distraction. It was not his psychological disposition, and conflict was not part of his psychological fingerprint.

In one of our discussions, we had an in-depth conversation about the role of outsiders in his performance journey. He needed to understand that he will always have critics, naysayers, and detractors, but it is his responsibility to learn to limit the influence on him. To be successful, he would need to understand the impact of his environment on his overall perspective.

He is not the only one struggling, and often, the actions of others are nothing more than a reflection of their struggles. If he took it personally, which is very easy to do, he would start to carry the burdens of others instead of creating the glory of his success.

When people struggle, they often look for others to validate their angst, support in their misery, and reassurance that their pain is not because of their own doing. The more they suffer, the more they recruit psychological support from others. Unfortunately, you often get caught up in their drama, which will take away from your pursuits.

Why are we so motivated to find comfort in another's misery?

Why does another's struggle make it easier to handle than our own?

What is wrong with merely accepting our efforts as our journey?

The Residents of Suckville

You are not alone in Suckville. And that is the problem. Your misery only enhances others' connection to you. It makes them feel better and, unfortunately, makes you feel better, too – over the short term. They become somewhat attracted to your struggle to ease their suffering or feel better by helping you. Nothing is ever done without a benefit of some kind, so their actions are not done without getting something back in return.

One word of advice – be careful sharing your vision and desires with those in your circle. Former NFL player and current motivational speaker, Trent Shelton, summarized it perfectly when he said, "the bigger you get, the smaller your circle should get."

When you share your vision, do not fall into the trap of hoping for their validation to support yours. You will not get it. You are more likely to get biases and insecurities of others than the truth.

Who are the residents of Suckville that work hard to make sure you stay there and like it? I have found there are five different types of people who want you to stay stuck in Suckville and do not want you to succeed.

The Naysayers

A couple of years ago, my college-aged daughter set up an appointment with her academic counselor in the Business School at her university. She was earning a business and marketing degree and was planning on attending law school. My daughter is by no means perfect, and I am not delusional to think that she is the next most magnificent gift to our society. Still, she is very hardworking, very entrepreneurial, and very motivated. Heck, she started a profitable business while in school and was often the subject of some of her professors' discussions. But I digress about my wonderful daughter.

Anyway, she set up an appointment with her counselor about getting course credit for an internship over the summer. She had earned an internship with a Federal Judge, and by working behind the scenes all summer, she thought she could get an elective credit like many of her colleagues. As she presented her case to her counselor, the counselor went on to destroy her dreams. If the counselor had not repeated the same things to my wife in a follow-up conversation, I would not have believed it.

The following is a brief recap of the conversation:

My daughter: “I would like to receive credit for my summer internship. How do I do that?”

Counselor: “Why would you get credit when they are not paying you? That seems like you made a bad decision to accept an internship when you are not getting paid. We do not provide any course credit in those circumstances because I feel that it is wrong for a company to take advantage of you like that.”

My daughter: “I thought it would be a great experience to shadow a Federal Judge, a female, who has experienced a great deal of success and will be retiring soon, so I think she will have some great guidance for me. Plus, I don’t know how to get paid because it is the Federal Government.”

Counselor: "You want to go to law school? You know how many girls come to my office, tell me they want to go to law school, and then do not have what it takes? It is not about dressing pretty. If you think this experience will help you, you should spend more time studying and not take that internship. It is a waste of time, and honestly, it is not likely you will make it through law school."

As you can imagine, my daughter left in tears. Did I mention that the business school counselor was a female too? And my daughter graduated with nearly a 3.8 GPA in Marketing while managing a severe case of Crohn's Disease and running a profitable business that she could live off when she graduates? She could learn many things to do better, and that was why she searched for this internship. And yes, she completed an internship.

Here is the deal – some people would prefer to break you down and destroy your hope than encourage you. I call them Naysayers.

The Naysayers are so common, yet you rarely realize they are around you. You probably think that they are your friends, family, and supporters who have a knack for pointing out the "reality" of the situation. When challenged, they say they are just honest about your play and what you need to improve, even though they lay out a bleak future. Why are they focusing on the difficulty and negativity of your situation? You must understand their motivation.

Naysayers cannot see a positive future because they began to accept Suckville as their long-term residence. Naysayers doubt their own ability to push through the different challenges in their journey and transfer that doubt onto you for factors outside your control. Their insecurities become your responsibility.

Think about those in your life who will tell you that they want you to succeed, say all the right things, but as soon as you struggle, they highlight fifty reasons why you cannot overcome the challenges.

How do they make you feel? Initially, not that great. But over time, you will probably start to agree with them and buy into the increasing difficulty of breaking free from your struggles.

Naysayers are not bad people, and they ultimately mean well. Their issue centers around their misery and the inherent fear that you will progress further than they could. Doubt drives their decisions through each aspect of their performance.

Their doubts are not your responsibility. You must learn to protect yourself from the subconscious barrage of doubt and negativity. If you are not careful, you will not realize your perspective has soured, and you begin to see opportunities as increasingly more difficult. To protect yourself, learn to internally challenge their arguments as if you were in debate class, seeing the weakness of their argument and countering it with supporting evidence.

The Downtroddens

Imagine going to the county fair with your friends and playing every game in the arcade, only to lose every game you play. Despite the allure of the stuffed animals hanging above the ring toss, there comes the point that investing more money to win an unwinnable game becomes an irrational decision. Continuing to press forward with reckless abandon, hoping the next game will be your breakthrough, would likely be ridiculed by everyone in your group.

In this example, we quickly learn that losing is the norm, not winning.

Losing is a learned experience. At the outset of the competition, you had hope and a positive attitude. At some point, you crossed the line that losing is the norm.

You have a group of people in your life who accept losing as the standard and are unable to see success. I call them Downtroddens. They are like the character Eeyore in *The Adventures of Winnie the Pooh.*

If all you have ever done is fail, why would you expect anything different?

Downtroddens believe success is elusive, and the game consistently punishes those who try. It is easier to protect against the risks than put yourself out there to succeed. It is a dangerous world, so why even try?

Downtroddens allow their failures to define their identity. They are losers, not as people, but in the challenges of life, they invariably lose. Why should they try to achieve more? In their perspective, they have already determined the outcome as a failure.

You do not have to adopt their view of the world. You do not have to see failure as inevitable. If you were to see everything leading to failure, then you would validate your doubters' beliefs.

What is the worst thing a Downtrodden can see?

You have success when they could not see success as a possibility.

That is the ultimate struggle for a Downtrodden. It pains the Downtroddens at their core because if they were truly successful, it would have been them having success. Instead, they have failed so many times that it becomes a habit to come up short. It does not matter what you try or how hard you work; the outcome is always predetermined for a Downtrodden.

Deep down, Downtroddens want you to fail. Because what it takes to succeed can be significant, they believe your pursuits are illogical and wasted energy. Their opinions of your potential are not personal; they just reflect their perception of the world.

Your success scares them, but primarily because of what it means about themselves. You do not have to carry their burden, however. You must protect yourself from what they believe and establish your reality. The best thing to do is thank them for their opinion and perspective as you move forward with a positive mindset.

The Fearfuls

I know you can relate to the friend in your life who has that tremendous knack for identifying absolutely everything that could go wrong in life. It is like they have an exceptional talent for finding the struggle in anything, and worse, they are great at making you very aware of the same things they see. By doing so, they cause you to become more fearful about changing. I refer to them as Fearfuls.

Fearfuls work to identify the threats behind the scenes, deep in the darkness and out of your sight. They are different from Naysayers and Downtroddens because they do not doubt their abilities but instead worry about all the “what if's.” Fearfuls have a fantastic ability to identify all the barriers that impede success, and if you were not aware of what they are, you would be after speaking with them.

Fearfuls have the best intentions. Their anxieties limit their efforts.

While risk is determined by what you are willing to lose, Fearfuls prioritize risk over rewards.

They have not been beaten down by the game nor doubt their abilities—quite the opposite. Fearfuls want to succeed but are terrified of the risks associated with effort. Fearfuls tend always to hold back, saving something just in case. Fearfuls live with a great deal of regret and commonly second guess their decisions to gain more insight.

“Let me take my punishment now as opposed to fearing the punishment in the future” is the most accurate slogan for Fearfuls.

Fearfuls feel empowered when they are helping you. They want to do the right thing and giving you information about the dangers of competition seems logical. The problem comes when you begin to see the game through their lens. It is not accurate. They perceive the pains of the present are better than the potential pains down the road.

The future's uncertainty is often more threatening than what is known in the present, regardless of how uncomfortable it is now. Giles Strong, a researcher and academic from the Imperial College in London, England, studied the influence of "dread" of future discomfort on current actions. Throughout past experiments, people would rather take a bit of pain now instead of delaying suffering just in case future suffering is more painful. As a result, people dread the future more if they cannot experience the pain in the present.

In the study, 35 volunteers underwent an experimental scenario where they could choose to receive a small but uncomfortable electrical shock now to avoid the potential of more significant pain in the future (e.g., due to a painful dental procedure). The research question was how many would take the guaranteed discomfort now instead of rolling the dice of a future, uncertain punishment, and pain.

The results were interesting. Study participants preferred immediate pain instead of delaying the potential, but highly likely pain in the future. It seems it is always better to know than to anticipate, but as the possible pain intensified in the future, "dread" increased.

Those who dread potential dangers will do whatever it takes to avoid that pain. Their pain avoidance gets even more intense when they believe the punishments will be more painful in the future. If participants could educate themselves on the future pain and understand it in greater detail, the level of dread decreased. It seems that the fears in the mind are more significant in your imagination than.

Fearfuls want you to experience their dread, and the more they can educate you, the better they feel. You must be willing to educate yourself on the possibility and particulars of future risks and punishments. Their anxieties are not your fears.

Keep Fearfuls at a distance because you do not need to carry their anxieties into your competitions. Let them carry their own burdens.

The Jealous

There are people in your life who are jealous of your success. Every time you succeed, it pains them because they are not having the same success as you. They want you to fail so they can succeed.

The Jealous come in all shapes and sizes. I have seen coaches sabotage former players because they want a piece of their success, and parents make themselves the center of attention instead of the player. The Jealous destroy your journey because of their insecurities.

They want what you have so intensely that every success you have hurts them. The Jealous want you to fail solely to ease their pain.

Over time, their angst infiltrates your mindset as the negative breaks you down. You feel it and have to respond to it. With every reaction, you make it your responsibility. In doing so, they win. Their pain becomes an infectious disease.

Jealously often becomes resentment.

When resentment settles in, it can be destructive for all parties involved. Here is an example of this exact scenario. I was helping a new coach build her program at a mid-major university and deal with a staff member sabotaging the program's success. When the coach interviewed for the job, the university strongly suggested keeping the assistant coach on staff due to his recruiting connections and relationships with the returning players. He was an energetic personality and could motivate anyone to go beyond their limitations.

The problem was that he wanted the job. He had been overlooked because he lacked the organizational skills and commitment to the details necessary to be a head coach in a large college program. By staying on staff, the idea was he would be able to take on more responsibility and learn the necessary skills to be a candidate for upcoming head coaching opportunities.

My client involved him in nearly every major decision possible, bounced ideas off of him, and empowered him with opportunities to develop. He could not do it. He was so jealous of her advancement that he started to resent her efforts. It did not matter that he was essentially serving as a de facto head coach; his jealousy caused him to undermine any of her actions.

Being a head coach requires difficult decisions. My client had to address the resentment and sabotage immediately. She could not effectively lead a team if there was a jealous colleague destroying any progress. She had to fire him immediately.

His termination was not well accepted by the team, at least immediately. The team had lost their "players' coach" and their motivational catalyst. There were difficult moments she had to deal with, but over time, the players realized that his jealousy had undermined her.

Before the termination, she was frustrated with the team's performance. She doubted her ability as a head coach and struggled with her loss of motivation and insecurity. She had taken residence in Suckville, primarily because of his jealously. By eliminating the threat, she was able to reconnect with the process of coaching. Instead of trying to drive success to validate her worth, she could fully invest in her team.

The Jealous will resent your success and then resent the success of the next competitor that has prosperity. All the while never addressing their psychological pain of falling short of their goals. The fact they are in their Suckville devastation is not your responsibility.

The Easier Like It Is

Change can be very threatening for some, even though their

current personal approach is outdated, inefficient, or utterly ineffective. Some people would rather accept what they have now, even if it is less than what they could have in the future because the sacrifices are too steep. As a result, they resist.

Resistance is a common barrier for psychologists and therapists. At the start of any therapeutic relationship, clients have a desire to change. That is what brought them in as there was pain in their life, causing more and more problems. Once the original pain is relieved, they typically resist making other changes.

In your life, you have outsiders that feel that "it is easier like it is," and they do everything in their power to hold you back. They are happy with mediocrity and accept their fate because it is more predictable and does not require anything. Day in and day out, they know the plan, and they can trust the outcome. Even when they get stuck in Suckville, they seem to be okay with it. Striving for more is simply too risky for them.

Their fear is not your responsibility. You must identify those who feel it is easier to accept mediocrity instead of taking risks to achieve success and then protect yourself from their anxieties. For many, it is easier to accept the known mediocrity of the moment than to blindly venture out into uncharted territory. They cannot take the risk that things could get worse. Because there are no guarantees in life, some competitors simply learn to accept the pains of the present instead of risking the fears of the future.

Is that a risk worth taking?

If someone in your circle or on your team is too afraid to invest everything they have in their success, why should you listen to them? Those who feel that it is easier the way it is will spend their future trying not to change or evolve. With every new experience, they will do what it takes to prevent growth and attribute their successes to their ability to hold it together instead of the vulnerability required for lasting success. The future is always unknown.

Do not get held prisoner by another's fears.

Building Your Circle

The residents of Suckville bring all their insecurities to your experience. It is hard enough on your own, but when you must carry the burdens of struggling, it is the added weight you need to release.

Feeling natural emotions about another's success is universal. The journey towards prosperity is very challenging and sparks so many positive and negative emotions along the way. An essential perspective understands how your own experience is your personal experience. It is never more than that.

Removing the toxic attitudes from your life is often as important as bringing in additional support. Suckville should never be a growing population.

You need people and guides in your life. In my book, *The MindSide Manifesto*, I suggest you surround yourself with five core contributors. They are:

1. **Confidence Builders** – individuals who help build you up and help you see the strengths you possess inside you already.

2. **Competitors** – those you love to compete against and, in doing so, raise your game to new levels. You may get beat, but you will improve in the process.

3. **Colleagues** – those who have walked the same walk as you, so you can ask for nonjudgmental advice. Their goal is to solve the struggles and help you at the same time.

4. **Challengers** – they see the greatness inside you and demand it comes out. It may not be easy, it may be challenging, but the honesty and challenging nature will not stop until you reach the level of performance you can deliver.

5. **Critiquers** – like Challengers, critiquers deliver the directed feedback without much concern for your feelings. They are direct, sometimes harsh, and usually very accurate, willing to say what others fear telling you.

Each of these guides has a purpose, so finding them can be problematic in the place you are in your journey. It is easiest to surround yourself with those who make you feel good, and that is the risk of surrounding yourself with too many people.

Outsiders are not saviors. They all have their histories and challenges. Approach them with the motivation to learn and gain wisdom, not react to the problems in front of you.

Changing your environment is an internal and external thing. It is not simply moving away or changing teams. Seeing your struggles as teachable moments, eliminating the negative people from your environment, and leaving the game better than you found it will positively change your internal culture. That is how you change your circumstances and create a positive foundation for growth.

13

CHANGE YOUR PROCESS

I hear this a lot from players when interacting with coaches. "Coach, what is the process? You talk about it all the time, but what does that mean? I am so confused!"

The rest of the team agreed with the confused player. For so long, the team's coach would repeat the adage of "trust the process," but she never actually taught the players the foundations of the process. It was simply a phrase with as much structure as "you can do it!"

How do you practice? For how long?

What are your competitive mindset focus points?

How do you schedule rest?

Do you call for a full-court press after a made free throw or play zone?

Do you go for it on fourth down or punt? What part of the field will influence that decision?

What is your mindset after a missed shot? What do you like to do to motivate yourself?

All issues are simple aspects of a process. Just saying the words does not make it come to life. You must have one and live it, but how?

Skip Bertman and Nick Saban define process-oriented coaches. Both are arguably the most significant trailblazers in their sports. They have changed the way the games are coached and played. Bertman was my baseball coach at Louisiana State University (LSU) and won five national titles in ten years. He is in the College Baseball Hall of Fame and is easily considered one of the top college baseball coaches of all time. Upon retirement, Bertman became the Athletics Director (AD) at LSU, a significant promotion for a baseball coach in the multimillion-dollar world of intercollegiate athletics. Near the end of his tenure, he served as the AD while Coach Saban was the head football coach.

Bertman built his program around "The System," a performance philosophy that stressed the importance of doing the little things correctly, trusting the team dynamic, and not focusing on the outcomes. If you did the individual elements correctly, favorable results would follow. If you bucked the system, it would crush you. Every player in his program could recite The System because every Friday night in the off-season, we sat in meetings going through the Yellow Books.

In the spring of 2021, ESPN and the SEC Network released the documentary, *Hold the Rope*, which was an in-depth look at the life and coaching philosophy of Coach Bertman. I was fortunate enough to be in the documentary a few times to emphasize the importance of having a system, both mentally and physically. If you watch the documentary, you will gain insight into the power of a process and the Yellow Books.

Yellow Books were three-ring binders containing every element of the game that Bertman thought was important to succeed. The Yellow Books formulated The System in minute detail. Every aspect of how you practiced, competed, and trained was laid out in the Yellow Book so new players could catch on quicker than just going through the practices.

It was not how to pitch with more velocity, but instead, it explored the minuscule aspects of pitching, hitting, and game strategy. For instance, when pitchers attempt a pick off a runner, over 80% of the time, the next pitch they throw is a ball because they lose focus towards the hitter. Few players understand this and fall into the mental traps in the game. Not LSU baseball players. Bertman was meticulous, and he prepared his players for anything that could happen in the games.

The brilliance of Bertman's System was its simplicity. He created it as a high school coach and refined it each season through his college coaching career. The System guided every decision made in player development, game strategy, and organizational effectiveness. It was not just the philosophy but Bertman's discipline to the elements that made it successful.

Saban has a similar perspective as Bertman. Saban has won seven national titles as a college football coach at the time of this writing – one at LSU and six at the University of Alabama, including the 2021 National Championship. As the head coach of the Alabama football program, his teams have dominated college football, with three Heisman Trophy winners, and placed more players in the National Football League than any other program in the country. Saban has had unmatched success since he arrived on campus in 2007.

Saban relies on "The Process," where like Bertman, he focuses on doing everything you can do to the best of your ability and not focusing on the outcome. If you can be better at the details, victories follow. It is simple – do not leave anything for tomorrow. Commit yourself to become the absolute best you can be in everything you do and never stop.

I am fortunate. I played for five years under Coach Bertman, and I have worked in Coach Saban's program for eight years at the time of writing this book. I am the sports and performance psychologist for the University of Alabama and have been fortunate to learn from the best to coach and play for the best. My exposure to The System and The Process defines my perspective. I do not know anyone who has that combination as I do.

Bertman and Saban took advantage of human nature as well. When you focus on the details, you get ahead of your competition. Too many become obsessed with the sexy, shiny parts of their performance and ignore the easy things.

The effort it takes to succeed is never sexy. It is gritty, dirty, and exhausting. If you appreciate the details and stick with them, the details will produce powerful results.

The little things are harder to do because they are boring. Do them, own them, and commit to becoming great at the details. Your competition does not have the mental strength to do the same.

I have found that most will say they have a formal process, but the reality is few know it or adhere to it. Coaches often put fancy graphics with "The Process" emblazoned on the walls, right next to their mission statements, but few understand the elements that drive their performance. Saying "trust the process" is not the same thing as "trusting the process I have developed to dominate every challenge I face."

Big difference.

Every single competitor should have a process. Without that guidance, you are merely facing challenges with a random response, susceptible to short-term fixes instead of long-term development.

For the past few years, I have encouraged coaches to develop a Philosophy Binder to capture their systems and processes for developing players, dealing with game strategy, recruiting, and fundraising, among other things. Coaches must have their processes down on paper in an easily referenced book and updated annually to be effective. If they do not have it written down, it is not a process but rather a thought.

This past year, I started to do the same for my athletes. Your process is your formula for your success, and you should write each element of the process down for easy reference. I want you to create your personal Excellence Binder.

One of my players carries his Excellence Binder to every single team meeting. All of his notes are in the binder, game film review, and progress journal. He does not go anywhere without it. The results have been staggering as he set just about every single offensive record in his program. He told me that it allowed him to organize his thoughts and review his progress before games. It was not about his talent but his application.

The best athletes, teams, and companies adhere to a sound, strategic process. Circumstances can change, but their approach will be grounded in their tested and studied system for excellence. The problem is a system is hard to follow and gets quickly abandoned.

My Pleasure

Few organizations have the culture and organizational processes that can rival Chick-Fil-A. It seems that Chick-Fil-A has grown exponentially across the United States over the past 25 years. As a chicken restaurant, founder, Truett Cathy, wanted a fried chicken sandwich that could be consistent across his fast-food restaurants with exceptional service, in a clean store, and always with "My Pleasure!" It does not matter where you go to a Chick-Fil-A; each restaurant is consistent with the mission and vision. The reason is every employee must buy into the system driving the Chick-Fil-A company.

Chick-Fil-A competitors often try to emulate their strategy but fail because they only implement select aspects of it. They fail to do the one important thing –to be consistent with the entire process.

In 2019, Popeye's Louisiana Chicken launched a social media "war" with Chick-Fil-A over chicken sandwiches. For years, Chick-Fil-A's chicken sandwich had been the industry favorite, without much competition. Popeye's was ready to challenge that. It was a bold strategy, but Popeye's had nothing to lose trying to steal market share.

Popeye's social media strategy drove an overwhelming response into their stores to release their robustly flavored fried chicken sandwich. Cars were lined up in the drive-throughs, even backing up regular traffic adjacent to their stores. Unfortunately, Popeye's stores could not deliver on-demand. The corporate offices of Popeye's had to stop sales of the chicken sandwich. An absolute disaster!

Popeye's then added the chicken sandwich back to the menu and had to stop sales again. Stores got overwhelmed, and customers started posting videos online highlighting the chaos in the stores. Because they could not handle the increased attention and demand in restaurants, all the positive momentum was destroyed.

In the end, Popeye's had a dramatic increase in social media interactions and a very nice bump in revenue. From that perspective, the strategy worked. Unfortunately, it also showed that the organization was not prepared to handle the increased attention, demand, and even struggles.

Popeye's did not have a consistent process like Chick-Fil-A. In fact, with all the attention and demand, Chick-Fil-A never broke down. Their stores just continued plugging away, serving customers, and trusting their process. Sure, Chick-Fil-A probably sold more chicken sandwiches because of the social media attention, but they created their method to handle similar business surges.

You must develop your process around your strengths. You cannot build your approach solely to avoid stress or enhance your protection against struggle. If you do not build your process to be on the offensive, it is no longer an advantage but instead a safety net.

Your Excellence Binder

A process does not solve every problem you will face, but having one is better than not having one. Your recipe for success must give you the familiarity of your skills and mental approach to trust when things get more challenging. Write down your system, or you will forget it. It has to be tangible and concrete.

A rock-solid process is formed by understanding what makes your approach unique, your skills an advantage, and your psychological fingerprint powerful to face each challenge. It is refined over time, hardened by periods of stress and struggle.

Your process needs friction to become stronger.

It is not created and then trusted.

It is trusted, applied, refined, and then applied again.

Over and over again.

That is how you develop a robust process.

I want you to write your process down and keep it in a binder for frequent reference. Each year, review your binder and add things you learned that could help you improve and eliminate any clutter from your process. I have always believed that it is not concrete enough for you to follow if it is not written down.

Here are the four critical foundations of your Excellence Binder:

1. Wants and Desires

What do you want?

What is it in your deepest desires that you want to accomplish, achieve, and have in your life?

On September 12, 1962, President John F. Kennedy boldly stated that the United States government would lead an initiative to put a man on the moon within a decade. In his speech at Rice Stadium in Houston, Texas, President Kennedy declared that the United States would not only go to the moon but successfully bring the astronauts home safely. Even though it was not easy, the fact that it was hard was why it was essential to do it.

Imagine if President Kennedy told the American public that he would maybe like to go to the moon. Could he have rallied the various agencies to allocate time, money, workforce, and human lives because he kind of wanted to do this?

Absolutely not. It took conviction and a clear understanding of what President Kennedy wanted to achieve to get buy-in from all parties involved in the mission.

I have found time and time again that competitors who are struggling fail to admit to themselves what they want. I am not sure why we have evolved to such a spot that saying what you desire is viewed as dangerously self-centered by others. The result is tragic – a competitive journey lacking the navigational direction and fight to make greatness happen.

Simply saying you do not want to struggle anymore is not a desire that drives results. It only creates more struggle.

Not suffering as a competitor is not worth the extra hours of training.

Earning the next contract is.

Being the starter and dominating are.

Reconnecting to your joy in the game, the beauty of the battle, and fine-tuning your grittiness are essential.

"Doc, I don't want to struggle anymore!"

That is significantly different than, "Doc, I want to own my process and go all-in on the details and see how far I can go in the game!"

Look at those two statements and ask yourself how you feel reading them. One is purposeful, and one is preventative.

I want you to be determined and driven by the desire to achieve your goals.

You must connect to what you want in your life in every aspect.

I want you to write down everything you want in each aspect of your life – personal, professional, academic, etc. Simply write them down on a piece of paper and list them as they come to you. Nothing is too outlandish or wrong to write down. Not everything is achievable or feasible within a timeframe, but if you do not write it down, then how will you allow yourself the freedom to fight for what you want to accomplish?

After you list the individual desires, look at the listing and look for any common trends or groupings. More than likely, your wants will fall into three major categories: Athletic/Job Desires, Personal Desires, and Family Desires. Relist each of them and consolidate them under those three categories. It will help you understand where to direct your energy and efforts.

It is time to stop living for others and seeking validation from coaches, parents, and fans. You cannot allow the opinions of others to take control of your process.

You cannot merely succeed because others want you to have success. You must want it for yourself!

For every want and desire, there are barriers to success. Your barriers are much more manageable when you can identify them instead of trying to ignore the potential of impediments.

Every aspect of life has barriers and impediments to success. You can have the best intentions, but your progress will stop if something prevents you from going forward. You must face those barriers directly or find an alternative path.

On the backside of the paper, where you listed your WANTS, write down the BARRIERS that may prevent you from achieving them. Trust me; you are aware of them, so write them down to work through them.

The best embraces the challenges to find solutions. Instead of feeling frustrated and stuck, the most successful entrepreneurs, coaches, and athletes use the angst as motivation to solve the puzzle. All competition, for that matter, is really like a puzzle, and when you balance the wants and desires with the barriers and impediments, it becomes a beautiful challenge. In working through them both, you gain insight, sometimes in an instant.

When working on a complicated puzzle, you likely have a strategy to complete the puzzle. You may organize the pieces by colors or by specific aspects of the puzzle. You know what you want to accomplish, but sometimes it is difficult to figure out what pieces fit the puzzle. You may put complex pieces to the side or try to work in a particular section, but the perspective of every piece is the key to doing the puzzle.

The pieces only fit when it is the right time for them to fit into the larger picture. You can try and force it, but it will not work. When you have the puzzle piece you think should fit, you must look at it from different angles to shift your perspective. Only when it clicks in your head does the piece fit. The funny thing is that once it fits, it is as if you should have seen it the whole time. It is perfection.

Your wants and desires are the same way. If you create the picture of what you want, it comes down to working the individual pieces to achieve it. Sometimes you must change your perspective, and other times, be patient. But keep working towards the solution.

Know your wants and desires. Appreciate your barriers. Work through both.

2. Habits, Decisions, and Choices

Success leaves clues.

Struggle leaves destruction.

Failure leaves scars.

James Clear, author of the bestselling book *Atomic Habits*, extolled the power of small actions and thought processes essential to drive success. Charles Duhigg wrote *The Power of Habit*, and Gretchen Rubin authored *The Four Tendencies*, both centered on similar habits.

Your habits drive your behaviors. For every action, you have something that triggered it. If that trigger is consistent enough over a given period, the behavior will continue, even after the trigger is removed. Habits are then formed when the behavior exists without much effort to trigger it. What are those habits? The small details and actions that drive elite performance.

The most successful individuals separate themselves from

everyone else by having excellent performance behaviors. Those actions are rarely sexy, complicated, or mysterious. What makes them valuable is they are driven by choices – to do it or not. It is as simple as that.

But what drives habits? If they are so simple, why do you struggle to break away from the negative patterns, get lazy, or procrastinate? It should not be hard to understand the simple formulas written in those books, published in success magazines, and widely shared on podcasts, right? So, what is wrong with you?

Nothing.

It is easy to look at patterns of behavior as if what you do lives in a vacuum, protected from the distractions of your world. If you execute the proper habit, you are a superstar. If you do not, you are a worthless loser who does not understand the principles of behavior. But how do you separate emotion, motivation, anxiety, struggle, and apprehension into the purest models of habitual behavior?

That is where the simplistic models seem to fail.

It is never "all or nothing."

What you focus on drives your choices. It does not matter if it is positive or negative, constructive or detrimental. Those choices made in the passing minutes of each day drive decisions and influence actions or habits. What you do is rarely automatic as the most effective measures must be intentional – or where you direct your attention.

This point may appear in contrast to the books written on habits, but it is not. This perspective is just a different way to look. Each theory driving the understanding of habits shows that minor actions drive more significant results, and your viewpoint drives those actions. You must understand that those who have great success do not see positive progress without directing their attention to the immediate task at hand.

It is not happening outside their awareness.

Success is not magical.

Progress is about their choices.

A choice is where you choose to direct your attention. It is either what you decided to focus on or distract yourself. Those choices are smaller mental efforts and have smaller rewards or consequences. But they drive actions.

Choices are:

- Paying attention in class
- Going to training sessions and giving effort
- Calling your coach or trainer to schedule a training session
- Focusing on your successes instead of your struggles
- Reading and journaling about progress
- Thinking about where the ball is going to go before the play
- Listening to the message of your coach instead of the tone
- Packing your clothes and food the night before, so you are not rushed in the morning
- Doing your homework instead of waiting until the last minute
- Selecting healthy foods instead of highly processed snacks or meals

- Focusing on the next play and not the mistake on the previous play
- Showing up early

As you can see, those choices drive subsequent actions, push results, and do not take much effort. Your choices build to your next choices, which causes your following actions.

Choices are the spark that lights the fire, catalyzing your growth.

But choices are not easy.

There are specific factors that can impede "correct" choices, such as fear, uncertainty, low self-belief, and low motivation. Each moment in your life creates a choice point, where you have to make the small effort to do the positive action with delayed gratification or take the short-term option that may be easier, more fun, and feel good at the moment, but not produce the long-term results. The positive choices rarely feel good or have the reward in the heat of the moment.

Uncertainty disturbs your ability to make proper choices because the potential risk influences short-term safety instead of other long-term decision-making. It creates wrong choices because you get overwhelmed by options and lack definitive direction. For many, the additional mental clutter impedes action because of paralysis by analysis. The more uncertainty, the harder it is to focus on "correct" choices because all you want is to avoid the discomfort associated with not knowing the future.

When you get distracted, you must regain your awareness and focus on building positive momentum. Do not get angry about getting distracted. Use that energy for the next positive choice you make. By breaking the negative chain of distractions, both internal and external, your choices start to build Habits and Decisions.

If choices are the little things, decisions are the more significant moments of mental focus that create long-lasting action. If choices create a ripple, decisions develop waves. Decisions require more effort, more attention, and more significant consequences, both good and bad. Choices build to put you in a position to make the decisions that can change your course. Choices can be in the moment, but decisions take time.

Decisions are:

- What team you decide to play for.
- What coaches you hire to train you.
- Making changes to your team, technique, or process.
- Developing a training plan for the off-season.
- Changing equipment.
- Taking a new job or position in your company.
- And so on.

The choices you have made get you in a position to make the decisions that chart your future. While choices often seem meaningless, they set the stage for decisions to enhance impact. Without the series of often seemingly empty choices, you would never be present in the exact moment for your decisions to hold importance.

It is easy to struggle with the enormity of decisions and struggle to commit fully. Anything worth fighting for must be evaluated from every single perspective.

When you are weighing the options of making an important decision, you must consider:

- The advantages and benefits of making the decision,

- The consequences and disadvantages of making that decision,
- The advantages and benefits of not making the decision,
- And, the disadvantages and consequences of not making the decision.

In other words, what are the benefits and costs of either doing something different or staying the same?

Both have advantages and disadvantages that will influence your decisions, so you need to see things from every perspective. It is easy to see the risks and benefits of changing and ignoring the pros and cons of staying put.

A great way to look at the influence of Decisions and Choices would be how an athlete decides who to hire as their private training coach. In today's performance world, there are thousands of coaches touting their services to prospective elite athletes. It must be hard to decide who to use and understand the motivation behind that decision.

Imagine two scenarios.

In the first scenario, a player decides on a friend to train with limited training in a non-demanding environment. The player does not have the same level of accountability and can show up when they want because the friend is not that busy. The player's daily choices are not held to standards of excellence, and over time, their training level shows a lack of commitment. The player saved some money and did not have to leave town to train.

In scenario two, the player researches the coach and facility that have produced some of the best performances in their sport. The player decides on a facility in the upper Midwest that fosters a focused training environment, eliminating all outside distractions for the off-season. During this time, the player's choices start getting more productive and effective. The decision required the player to move away from their family for a significant period and immerse themselves in training, and it was costly. The player chose to see it as an investment into his/her future.

Which decision would increase the likelihood of the player performing at an elite level when the season started?

Which decision fostered a sense of contagious choices?

Decisions are not easy. They often require an "either/or" approach, and you have to be fully committed to those decisions, even if they seem inconsequential. Your choices may have more variability associated with them, but decisions have a more prolonged impact.

The most important consideration when making a big decision is what you have to do next. What must you consider and the conditions relevant for my next decision? Can you respond to it?

That is where actions and behavior come into play. What you do and how you do it matter. Decisions do not lead to actions; choices do. Choices build actions you do repeatedly and form into habits.

Your actions create the process because it is what is most observable, and the choices lead to the decisions that propel those habits. The more you do them, the less time and mental energy it takes to make the choices, decisions, and actions. Those habits become automatic. In doing so, they become very powerful.

Habits are:

- Routines and activities completed consistently
- Journaling every day at the same time
- Planning your training or activities each morning

- Giving thanks and expressing gratitude
- Following a schedule

The fact is this – habits drive your performance because they do not take as much mental energy, allowing you to focus on adapting and responding to challenges. It is hard to be fully present and drive positive action if you are not mentally organized, lack consistency in your day, and surround yourself with chaos. Habits establish a solid foundation to sustain through good and bad times.

Unfortunately, over time, habits are at risk of breaking down—motivation lapses. The urgency causing you to make choices more hastily, stress influences your ability to make crucial decisions, and your actions become more preventative. Everything loses its importance. When they become so automatic, they risk falling out of your immediate attention.

When motivation suffers, you have to refocus your attention on the choices you make. You have to use your energy for effective decisions instead of preventing mistakes or becoming stressed about your circumstances. Having a motivational lapse is expected, but what you do after that matters. This motivational lag period is how what you do becomes intentional actions, the next step of your process.

3. Critical Actions

During any competition, momentum can shift in an instant. In every game, the outcome seems to come down to a few critical moments that changed the course of play. Think about the moments in your own life that your course suddenly shifted and how things have been different ever since.

It is a dropped interception.

A missed bunt.

A turnover when the momentum was in your favor.

A missed fairway or short putt.

The moment was right there for you to take the right action, and oops, you missed it.

The choices, decisions, and habits ready you for the bigger stage, but it is your time to take the step with confidence and purpose when it matters. These moments are what I call Critical Actions.

Throughout your process development, you must be mindful of what skills, both mentally and physically, you have to meet the moments. You must understand that in the face of challenge, ambiguity, and uncertainty, the natural mental default is protection against risk or failure.

Your mind wants to prevent further loss and damage, so it seems to generalize or rationalize the "not so bad option" as protection. But that does not bode well for the competition. Coming in a "not terrible" position is dramatically different than winning. Your process must be built around actions to achieve and not a mentality to prevent feared outcomes.

Often, your fear of further struggle takes over, and instead of making the right choices, you protect against more difficulty. You create what you fear, but you make it worse with the frustration and regret that amplifies the struggle following the failure.

You must face the worst-case scenario with directed action. There will be no invitations, only opportunities.

There are two major types of Critical Actions to face opportunities:

1. **Intentional Action**

   Do not do something if you are not all in on doing it.

Half-assed efforts result in half-assed outcomes. You want to drive results to achieve the most you can, requiring that level of intentional action.

One of the most significant risks for competitors in today's world is not giving 100% intentional effort on the task at hand. Why? Because it seems to be a protective mechanism.

Here is my thought process – if you give everything you have, your blood, sweat, and tears into something and come up short, the only conclusion you can make is that maybe you are not good enough. As a result, you hold back, giving you an excuse if you fail. But if you cannot find a way to give all that you have, you do not give yourself much of a chance to be successful. Your protection does nothing more than make you fail. When you hold back your effort, all you are doing is protecting your ego.

It is not the only conclusion you can make if you come up short. Assuming you do not have "what it takes" is irrational and reactionary. Numerous factors are influencing the outcome, but your self-esteem and self-image cannot be rational under pressure.

Intentional Action requires you to give all that you have towards the challenge. It is about being driven, determined, and relentless. There has to be a purpose of achievement and a determination to finish the job. If you lack either of those, you are just going through the motions.

The daily choices you make that build the habits for success prepare you for the moments of action. You are not overexposed or unprepared. Give yourself the freedom to achieve and work through the chaos.

The intention is often verbalized but rarely executed. I have found that it is hard to be so focused on achievement that nothing else matters. Golfers rarely lock in mentally to be so focused on the intention of the shot. Pitchers rarely elevate their mindset to be 100% clear on the pitch. Basketball players rarely get their tunnel vision to make a three-pointer.

The reason is the lack of intentional direction. You get caught up in the clutter, stress, and risks and fail to choose where to focus. Believe it or not, it is that easy. You cannot ignore distractions, but you must decide to redirect your focus to what matters the most. Over time, you get better and better at directing your attentional focus into intentional action. It is a skill.

2. Critical Action Response to Error (CARE)

Throughout competition, errors happen. It does not matter if the mistake occurred because of a lack of focus, preparation, or execution. Once the error happens, all that matters is the next choice or action.

The mind is hardwired to protect you from threats, and any error only intensifies your protection. Your mind would rather forego success in favor of not getting worse. That is why the action you take after a mistake is critically essential.

I listened to a Major League Baseball pitcher talk about his routine after giving up a home run. It was inevitable that he would give up one home run throughout a season, so the pitcher decided to have a plan for precisely that moment. As a former pitcher, I can personally attest to the anger, disappointment, and sometimes shame of giving up a home run. The opposing team celebrates at home plate while the hitter

> slowly rounds the bases. You cannot pitch again until the home plate umpire finally throws you a new baseball (because the last one ended up over the fence). The natural tendency is to use anger which would frequently lead to the pitcher overthrowing his pitches to the next hitter.
>
> That cascade of events is not your process.
>
> As a result of the changed process, the pitcher will lose command and struggle to get outs. The more they struggle, the faster additional problems show up. This Major League Baseball pitcher did not want to allow one mistake to compound into a terrible inning, so he planned for the following action after the home run.
>
> In doing so, he put the home run behind him (e.g., it was not a good pitch, but it was the only one today) and focused physically on the next pitch (e.g., commit to hitting the outside part of the plate). He took control mentally by choosing to let go of the recent past and focus on the following action.
>
> You will make mistakes, even if you are 100% prepared for the challenge. Competitive results are never entirely in your control. But how you face the next choice or action after a mistake is. It takes CARE – a Critical Action Response to an Error – to drive results.
>
> Your process should have plans for after error actions. Do not wait for a mistake to occur to figure it out. Build it into your process and make it an essential element of it.

You determine the value of your process by the actions you take in both simple and challenging times. Success requires you to devote your energy to what you can control, and that is always your choices and then actions. It is easy to get distracted or lose motivation, get obsessed with the results, or fear the consequences, but what is most important is you direct your energy into the actions that matter the most.

4. Values – Internal and External

Maya Angelou, the brilliant poet and civil rights activist, famously opined:

> *"I've learned that people will forget what you said, people will forget what you did, but people will never forget how you made them feel."*

Angelou made an amazing impact on humanity.

You can do so much for people, but if you make them feel inconsequential, unimportant, or angry, they will never forget how you made them feel. It is the same for feeling empowered, confident, and successful. Your values define your legacy.

Every great process should be constructed with the exit in mind. Did you do it the right way? Treat others respect? Help them in their struggle?

Do not construct your process to take advantage of another or cheat the system. That is not a process.

Your values should be built with an internal and external compass, directing your beliefs on what you want your impact to be on the game, how you treat others, and how you contribute to society.

When developing your process, look beyond your struggles and successes. Look at the values that you feel you should have for yourself and the greater community.

Internal Values

Some factors important to consider for your internal values are:

- Dependability
- Reliability
- Who you are responsible for
- Willingness to learn
- Coachability
- Trust
- Service of others
- Honor those who came before you and the ones who will follow you
- Faith and Spirituality
- Forgiveness
- How you treat others
- Respect for others' dreams, backgrounds, and identities
- Guidance and Mentorship

Consider how you want your internal values expressed in the world. Your actions and behaviors serve as a window into your values. What is important is how those values drive your efforts to positively impact the world, your friends, and your family.

External Values

When exploring the concept of external values, I consider it from a perspective of who you want to associate with and how the world will view you. While you cannot control how others form their opinions of you, those you associate with tend to cast a significant presence.

External values reflect how you construct your team, the type of coach you want, and how you approach the competitive environment, so they express your internal values to the world around you. They must work in concert, or you risk being out of balance personally and professionally.

It does not matter how fantastic your uniforms are, how elite your training center is, or how many banners and trophies are displayed. What matters is the collective group challenges each player to be better and demonstrates a culture of excellence. Your competition will see and feel that excellence.

I have worked with players who have spent seasons relegated to the bench and played very little, while the player ahead of them on the depth chart becomes an All-American. While it is frustrating for the player to wait their turn, I challenge them to build their internal and external values.

Can they continue to root for their team and other players, even though they are not playing?

Can they learn through observation and immersion while at practice and use it for the opportunity to present themselves?

Can they train at practice, hip-to-hip with the All-

American, even though they may not play a game this season?

At The University of Alabama, our football players must deal with this every year. With each recruiting class, the talent levels of the players seem to exceed previous incoming classes. The current roster has elite talent AND experience in the system. The ability and talent level on the bench could start at 95% of the teams in the country. Because external values are passed down through generations, older players who have waited their turn are ready to take over when their time comes.

For the younger players, it is crucial to educate them on using each practice to challenge themselves, learn from the best, and contribute to the team training sessions. As a result, the culture becomes a training ground for greatness.

Josh Jacobs was the first-round pick of the Las Vegas Raiders in 2019. He was not highly recruited in high school and arrived at Alabama with little fanfare. Jacobs' upbringing was challenging as his family was homeless and left without regular meals and a safe bed to lay their heads on. It inspired a deep desire to succeed for Jacobs. He used every day as an opportunity to grow, prove to the doubters he had the tools, and learn from the greats ahead of him.

Jacobs was driven but patient. With each opportunity, he played very hard, showed immense toughness, and refined his skills. He was ready, focused on his process, and soaked up the program's values, which was why he chose Alabama in the first place.

It was the same way for me with LSU Baseball. In my first practice as a young freshman, I learned the importance of external values and the team's culture.

Although he eventually became one of my mentors, I was immediately put in my place by an All-American junior pitcher, Chad Ogea. He was tough, direct, and no-nonsense, and he intimidated me.

At my first practice, I could not retrieve a baseball hit out of the park in batting practice. At that time, all missing baseballs meant additional running for the pitchers after practice. No one wanted to run extra after a five-hour practice. This baseball was stuck between two fences, and I would have to climb the two fences to retrieve the ball. I have never been a good fence climber. Ever.

At first, I gave it my best effort and ran back into the pitcher's huddle as the practice was winding down.

Ogea looked at me and asked, "Did you get the ball?"

"No, I couldn't get it. It is stuck in between the fences," I replied.

"Go try again," Ogea told me sternly.

I jogged back out behind the left-field fence, only to fail again. When I returned, Ogea asked me again if I had it.

"Man, I can't get it," I told him.

"Look, you have one choice – do it right or not at all. There is no in-between at LSU. We do things a certain way, so go out there and do not come back until you get the damn ball," Ogea barked.

Now, I was scared. I had to get the ball. I was a true freshman who was not being counted on for anything that season. I did not need enemies.

I ran back out to the fences, started climbing, and got

the ball. When I got back to the huddle, Ogea looked at me and said, "See, you could do it. We do not quit on ourselves here. You need to learn that."

The external values were instilled in me right at that moment. It was about living up to the standards established before I had arrived on campus.

That day changed my whole mindset. There was no halfway for me—no quitting.

Ogea was the winning pitcher in our 1991 National Title game, was drafted in the 3rd round of the Major League Baseball draft and won two games in the 1997 Major League Baseball World Series. He became my mentor, and I followed him around like an apprentice. While we are still great friends, there are times when I get around him, and my youthful anxiety sparks back up.

The standards of excellence in our program had been passed down with each generation of players. Ogea was mentored by Ben McDonald, the 1989 Golden Spikes Award winner (the college baseball equivalent of the Heisman Trophy) and the first overall pick in the Major League draft. McDonald was one of the greatest players ever to play college baseball. Ogea was a freshman when McDonald was a junior, his last season at LSU. McDonald later told me that when he was a freshman, the older pitchers sat him down and taught him the responsibilities and values of being an LSU Baseball pitcher. It was a responsibility for every player who followed. I did my best to mentor those who followed me too.

Patrick Coogan.

Eddy Yarnell.

Eddy Furniss.

Ryan Theriot.

Kurt Ainsworth.

Every single LSU baseball player who followed.

Coach Bertman established the values of LSU Baseball from the outset. The external values were more prominent than any single player in the program. As a player, you had to do your best to contribute to that culture, or you would be broken by it. Like Josh Jacobs, you could not fight the culture, the process, or the program's values. It was just too strong because each player felt a responsibility to carry it forward.

You must connect your internal values to your external values. The collective of your team's internal values will create an unstoppable culture. Do not resist larger forces. When you match those values up, you will start executing with greater ease and freedom. If you continue to resist, you will continue to struggle.

Your process is your foundation for success. The best coaches and athletes have spent years refining their processes. It may take years to optimize yours into a world-class system, but if you continue to invest in it, it will continue to perform.

When you struggle, you abandon your process to protect against the dangers of competition and adverse outcomes. You built your process to succeed, not protect. As a result, you become an equivalent to Popeye's – a competitor with the right intentions, unprepared for success, and terrified of failing.

Your journey to this point has provided you the evidence and ingredients to build a reliable process. It is your responsibility to develop your binder, become the leader through your mental darkness, and refine that process to manage the good, the bad, and the phenomenal. Without a process, you are doing nothing more than searching and guessing.

14

CHANGE YOUR EFFORT LEVEL

"The moment you give up is the moment you let someone else win."

— ***Kobe Bryant***

Member of the Naismith Memorial Basketball Hall of Fame

When was the last time you left a competition or training session truly exhausted?

I don't mean tired or simply worn out and sweaty. Giving your all until the point that you realized you had "absolutely nothing else to give" type level of effort.

Totally gassed.

If you have to think about it, the answer is NEVER.

What are you holding back?

You will not have a better scenario than the world you are in right now. Success will never invite you, and things will not suddenly become simple. What are you going to need to give everything you have for something that you desire?

You have spent an enormous amount of time and energy working towards a goal but holding back your power towards getting it done. It is time to start devoting all your life to getting this done.

What is stealing your energy?

You have three main domains in your life – your PURPOSE, where you have FUN, and where you COMPETE. It is impossible to be great at all three.

Your PURPOSE is your vocational impact on the world, who you impact, and where you invest. It takes significant time and effort to succeed with your job, your school, and balancing to be present with your family. Those wants you identified will be consistent with your PURPOSE. If they are not, then you need to reevaluate.

No one can go through life without FUN, but how much is too much? I want you to enjoy the social aspects of your life, the parties, and time away from your PURPOSE and your COMPETITION.

Finally, how do you COMPETE in your vocation and your competitive pursuits? It is more than just getting by and going through the motions. The competition takes every essence of you to be successful.

You have been spending too much time and energy on one and ignoring everything else. More than likely, FUN is taking far too much of your energy away from either your PURPOSE or COMPETITION. When it matters the most, you simply do not have enough to give you have not given what you think you should have available.

That is not the biggest problem, however. Not having it available when you need it is one thing, but the more concerning issue is having it but not letting it go. There is no more significant time than right now to give your all.

The Hold Back

I was standing at the baseline of a basketball court watching one of my college teams go through post-practice conditioning drills when I realized how easy it is for athletes not to give their "everything." The primary conditioning drill challenged the players to complete different running tasks within a specific time window. They would repeat the drill over and over with a short break in between the sets.

I watched one of the elite players dominate the drill. He was finishing with time to spare. It was not easy, but he rose to the challenge.

The other top player on the team continually finished the drill right on the time window. He would slowly start each repetition, pacing himself, and then rallied near the end to finish on time. Both players got the same result, a passing outcome, but the story of effort was completely different.

Player #2 was underperforming in games. It seemed that when the competition intensified, he disappeared or did not meet the moment. He continually got frustrated with the play calls and felt that he should be a more significant part of the game plan.

Player #1 became the focus of the game plan, and he rarely came out of the game. The team eventually named him captain.

The conditioning drill made sense. Player #2 was Holding Back. I met with him to figure out what was going on and why his conditioning seemed to be off. He told me that his training was not a big issue, but he was pacing himself because he did not like feeling tired and worn out at the end of the drill. The reality was he was terrified of getting deep into the conditioning drill and having nothing left to give.

But he never got to that point and never allowed himself to reach the end of vulnerability in this training. He was hanging on trying to make it and simply passed.

It was more profound than that, however. Player #2 was somewhat upset about not being voted a captain by his teammates. It was important to him that his colleagues saw him in a leadership role. But his effort told his teammates he was not giving them all he had. He was holding back, and the reason was he was terrified of failing. Yet, he was failing at multiple levels.

He wanted to succeed, but the fear was overwhelming. He did not want to feel that depth of failing, knowing he needed to do more, but he just could not muster the resources to get it done. It seemed better to hold back, realize he could be "good enough," and make it through each drill without the risk. But why was Holding Back such a risk?

The most significant risk to competitors is not an opponent but their self-doubt about their ability to succeed. When you give all you have and still come up short, it is hard to see anything other than the possibility that it may not ever happen for you.

"I may not be good enough."

"I do not think I will ever have success."

"Why am I falling so far behind the other players?"

Each reflects the corrosive properties of the fear of being inadequate. It is a hard truth to accept, so you fear it with great intensity. Your only protection against that fear from becoming a reality is to hold back effort. That is a performance safety blanket.

Holding back is a powerful act of resistance to the possible truths. Doing so just builds the ease of accepting your regret.

Every athlete must come to terms with this fear. You will never have total confirmation of your potential, and that is why you will never reach it. With each day falling short, you get better at holding something back. It becomes an automatic, subconscious choice.

Your past struggles prepare you for more challenges in the future. The scarred and traumatic memories of failures, frustrations, and disappointments amplify current challenges and bring the pain from the past into the present. As the discomfort of your struggle intensifies, your desire to escape the pain will limit your vulnerability and mental flexibility.

If you protect yourself from the possibilities of any result, you withhold your full capabilities. The game is not getting your best, and you are selling yourself short.

"I am better than that!

I am sick and tired of doing the same thing over and over and not getting any better.

I do not know how much longer I can do this without having any positive results!"

Statements like that are prevalent yet lack the vulnerability to face the fear of the future and self-doubt. Your effort must reflect your desire and not your anxieties. Your stresses are so much more potent than your wants, and they will hijack your mind. They will not let go. As a result, the only way to mentally survive is to go into full protection mode.

Why have you not gone "all-in" on your journey?

What are you so afraid of losing?

It would be best to become relentless in your desires, aggressive with your choices, and accepting all possibilities.

You have created the same struggles you fear because you are trying not to mess up. So why continue trying not to make mistakes?

Elite effort must be built around your determination, supported by your confidence, directed by your motivation, and evaluated according to the possibilities. To give everything you have for something you want is more than a simple choice. You must be ready to walk away disappointed, exhausted, and frustrated. There are no protections. The only things you have are your self-belief in your physical and mental abilities and the depth of your trust in yourself.

Your energy level gets freed up when you trust your process, accept the outcome, and become comfortable with your identity. You are not Suckville. You are only experiencing Suckville. The effort will be fostered by a series of factors, such as your self-determination, self-belief, self-powered actions, and your self-insurance. Let us review those factors:

1. Self-Determination

Effort flows like a roaring stream of water, going where momentum and gravity direct it to go. Water always finds a way to stay moving and can move its impediments if strong enough.

Effort must be directed towards a target. Your determination provides the direction. If the goal is to survive, you will not thrive. If the goal is to dominate, then you just might.

Effort will match that determination. Effort is dependent upon what you want to accomplish. Plain and simple.

You will not drive extra effort unless the outcome is something that you desperately desire. You will not work through the struggles if it is not worth sticking with it for a goal in mind.

Lions do not hunt unless they are starving. When lions become extremely hungry, they cannot afford to fail. The hunt consumes them. The goal is primary at that point.

Championship teams do not settle for simply being "in the game."

The greats do not measure their season by making it to a

championship game; they measure it by how they do in the final moments. For my program at LSU Baseball, being at the College World Series was not the goal. The College World Series was one step on what we set our sights on initially – winning the whole thing was our only goal.

Several years ago, former University of Alabama head strength and conditioning coach Scott Cochran walked into the locker room with the runner-up trophy from College Football Playoff from the previous year and smashed it in front of the team. It became a viral sensation online, but it reflected the intense desire of the entire program. The Alabama football team does not care about anything other than winning the biggest games. That is why they created their process in the first place.

I have never questioned a player who is honest with their desires. Do not be afraid to tell yourself what you truly want! You do not need to declare it to the world, but you can admit it to yourself and your inner circle and coaching team. I have never met a champion surprised by their success.

I had a player tell me they wanted to be in the Hall of Fame. He is now.

I had a player tell me they wanted to become an All-American. She became a three-time All-American.

I had a coach tell me they were going to build a championship program. He has – several times and at several different schools.

If you are willing to state it clearly, back it up with the effort to achieve it, then you may just reach it. But you must believe you can do it.

2. Self-Belief

It is hard to achieve what you do not believe, but you may not consistently achieve what you believe. That is the conflict.

Belief is so vital for a competitor because it is the core of the competitive psychological framework. Your self-image reflects your confidence in actions, trust in difficulties, and the summons of the energy necessary to persevere.

Belief is the oxygen for your fire. It feeds your determination from the inside out. You must work diligently to build your belief every day.

It is easy to focus on your shortcomings and get caught up in that dangerous cycle. The areas you struggle with do not have to be corrected to be successful. You have everyday things you just are not that good at, and that is okay. Your strengths overcome your weaknesses.

I have been a part coaching teams who get distracted by the glaring weaknesses and overlook strengths. The coaching team will lose focus on the total package and become obsessed with believing that their shortcomings are crushing their performance. It sounds logical to improve the areas causing some struggle, but the player starts investing more time fixing one problem and less time growing their strengths.

Their strengths are vital for a reason, and they know how to get better there. Even negligible improvements around your strengths can produce significant gains. With each small success around your strengths, you build more confidence and expand your self-belief.

When you chase your weaknesses, you are not mentally prepared to deal with the moments of confusion and frustration. It hurts your strengths and destroys what drives your performance.

Be you.

Believe in yourself.

Build a better you.

Do not ever stop.

Your belief is not a light switch. You must work on it daily. I recommend journaling, reading, affirmations, and anything else you can rely on to improve yourself. Do not chase your weaknesses. Build from your strengths.

3. Self-Powered

If belief is the oxygen that fans your fire, motivation is the gas fueling the burn. Motivation ultimately boosts your effort. Consistent with your self-determination, the importance is finding what fuels your drive.

It is always 100% personal.

Every great competitor has a reason for their motivation. They may not share it with anyone. Being a psychologist for elite competitors, I often gain insight into their motivational drive. It is rarely what fans or coaches see on the outside.

Great coaches get invited into the motivational engine from time to time because their players' trust them. You need positive influences and catalysts to push you forward. Use your team to help you. Find your motivational advantage.

Michael Jordan used the doubts of others to get motivated. As a kid, Michael's father would purposefully favor his older brother, just to motivate Michael. From an early age, Michael could not stand for anyone else to be favored over him, so it became an obsession to dispel the doubts of coaches, the media, and opponents.

Kobe Bryant was motivated by his desire to outwork his competition and be one of the best to play the game. He knew the investments he made in the gym gave him an advantage in fitness, technical excellence, and grittiness.

Jerry Rice played at a Division 1-AA football program, under the general public's radar, missed by recruiters of major college programs, and away from bright lights of the national media. As a result, he constantly questioned if his talent would be good enough. He did not dwell on it. Instead, he got after it. He committed himself to run precise routes, elevated his fitness, and trained in southern Mississippi's brutal heat and humidity. Rice did not waste effort obsessing about his shortcomings. Instead, he spent his time and energy building a Hall of Fame portfolio.

World-renowned soccer star, Abby Wambach, developed an elite motivational drive after growing up in a household of older brothers. Every day was a competition and losing in a household of older brothers would never end well for Abby, so she refined her "refuse-to-lose" mentality that made her one of the world's best. For Abby, it was win or face the humiliation of losing. It did not matter that she was the youngest.

And so on.

The best competitors understand how to tap into that moment when they need it the most.

It is either an internal fire or an external drive, correct? Well, it is both, at different times.

I have heard over and over that internal motivations are the best and drive the most successful actions. Sure, in theory, when in a vacuum from the real world.

Your internal drive is critically important, but so are your external triggers. Things such as fear of letting others down, desire to be a world champion, or building a bank account up are great motivators. The problem is they do not last long. Buying into them is how you end up in Suckville.

The internal motivators must take over from the external triggers that start you on your journey. It is the give-and-take balance that drives success.

Your effort is determined by how you manage the balance between the different motivations.

4. Self-Insured

I feel like this is the section for the legal disclaimer – "All action requires risk. Take all considerations of potential risks before moving forward."

Risk is everywhere. There is nothing you can do to eliminate it. You have to find the balance between determination and risk and match your effort accordingly.

The evaluation of risk is a personal decision and determined through a conscious approach. What are you willing to lose?

How much discomfort are you ready to endure?

What are you willing to give up pushing forward?

Some competitors conclude through their risk analysis that the effort may cause future risk in their draft stock, coach's opinion, or opinions on social media. I can understand those conclusions. While many of those final risk assessments may seem trivial for outsiders, the most important thing is determining what is important to you – that is all that matters. All I ask is you try to see the risk from as many different perspectives and not just react to the difficulty.

Risk is mediated by experience. Every time you compete, you gain wisdom that you can use for the next competition. You become more efficient with increased knowledge.

The more success you have, the more risk increases too. There is not much psychological risk of being mediocre. There is a risk coming in last, such as losing your job, but you rarely consider the volatility of success.

It is hard being a top-ranked team. You get everyone's best shot.

It is risky being lead the whole game or tournament. If you win, everyone thinks you should. But if you struggle and lose, you are a choker. Unfortunately, success complicates.

You must apply effort despite the presence of risk. There will never be a competition where you are entirely immune to the negative consequences. Unintended events arrive, and frustrations will build. Things change in an instant.

Risk is fluid.

Nothing is ever guaranteed or safe.

Does that scare you away or fire you up?

The Risk of Judging Effort

I want to add a word of caution with effort. Be careful judging another person's level of energy. You do not see the intention or the struggle below the surface.

I have taken numerous calls from coaches and parents about one of their competitors who "seems to quit on their effort when it gets hard." That statement gives me great concern because I have yet to have an athlete who says they give up when it gets overwhelming.

It is the opposite.

When struggle intensifies, and you get stuck in Suckville, it is natural to try harder. Many times, the harder you work, the more you will struggle. You are trying so hard that it looks like you give up.

This phenomenon is like starting your computer and opening every application you have at one time. The working memory and processor will be working so hard that every request will get bogged down. It looks like your computer is just sitting there, but it is working way too hard behind the scenes.

Do not judge another's effort because you cannot see what is going on behind the scenes. More than likely, they are working way too hard.

15

CHANGE YOUR QUIT MOMENT

"Our greatest weakness lies in giving up. The most certain way to succeed is always to give it one more try."

\- ***Thomas Edison,*** *Inventor*

You will never know how far you must go until you have no choice but to continue forward. It can be daunting to think about the struggles you have been through and the uncertainty of what you will face in the future, but what choice do you have? You cannot quit on your journey, and you surely cannot quit on your dreams.

Everyone has a quit threshold. There comes the point when the sacrifices are no longer worth it, the uncertainty gets too big, and the struggle too intense to keep pushing forward. Once you hit that moment and make a choice to stop, there is no going back. You must live with the consequences.

I have not met many competitors who prematurely quit who felt the time was the right time. Most regret their decision and pity the ease of making the decision. Those tough choices are justified by emotional reactions and rationalized by selective memories. You cannot quit on yourself.

There are times that you feel you have no more left to give. You always have more. Stop worrying about how hard it is and how much farther you have to go—those do not matter.

What does matter is summoning everything you have to give and giving all of it.

There is always more in your tank.

The Fork in the Road

Throughout your journey, there have been decision points that have influenced your overall trajectory. Some have been significant, and others have been seemingly inconsequential. Each has influenced the position you are in today.

When in Suckville, your ability to see the consequences of your decisions becomes clouded. It is hard to see the horizon when you are so focused on your feet. That is the unfortunate truth.

I had a professional golfer near the end of his professional career and struggling with the emerging reality that he may have to retire. He had not reached his goal of making it to the PGA Tour despite having moderate success at different levels of professional golf. He had watched his college teammates succeed on Tour, had to spend time answering questions from friends why he was still missing his goals, and worse, put in so much effort without much in return. The impending decision was looming on him.

The issue was not really about life after golf. He was from a family who ran a successful business across multiple generations. If he returned to the family company, he could earn a very nice living. Travel would be limited, and he could spend more time with his children.

On the surface, it looked like a viable alternative to the long days and empty nights as a journeyman professional golfer.

The problem was not a big decision. Every day, it was the little choices, how much would he be willing to invest in the work. He was always a grinder and never avoided the hard training days. But he began to feel he was going through the motions in his training. He was doing the work just to complete the work, not to enhance performance.

He had been so focused on the large fork in the road that he had completely overlooked the smaller choices each day. His fear of the uncertain future was crushing his performance. My question was this, "How can you decide on quitting the game when you are failing the daily quit questions?"

He was quitting on himself long before he realized. No doubt he wanted to succeed, but he did not appreciate how he was making it harder on himself to push through. By changing the decisions on the smaller quit moments, things started improving. Rather dramatically.

The most significant change happened with his overall mindset. Before we started working, he was struggling with intrusive thoughts during competition. After shots, regardless of the outcome, he found himself drowning in a barrage of negative thoughts. Out of nowhere, his mind would become very punishing to the point that he struggled to find any confidence. It resulted in a significant case of performance anxiety.

How can you compete against the best when you are your greatest opponent?

Every competitor comes to the point when escaping the pain of the continuous struggle must be considered. But have you ever thought that you might not have exhausted every option and there could be a different path forward?

The emerging fork in the road is not the problem. I want you focused on your daily choices.

We laid out the alternatives for my professional golfer, including his personal and professional life after his athletic career was to end. It was a great exercise to see the potential in the different options available. Seeing all the possibilities re-engaged him in his pursuits and reinvigorated him to make the more minor decisions with intensity and purpose. Success did follow, and he continues to play professionally.

The Quit Moment

Quitting is not a sign of weakness. Many times, it is a sign of strength. When you can establish your "out" in any venture or journey, it allows you to free the mind from the anxiety and pains that often consume your mental energy.

In Suckville, I bet you have been fighting against quitting for some time. It has probably popped up in your head, and you tried to fight against it. I understand it.

The more you resist quitting, the louder the voices will become trying to convince you to stop.

Stop fighting the fears.

I am not saying I want you to quit. I just do not want you to resist or fear quitting. If you chose to go in a different direction, just be all in for that direction. If you decided to push forward, just be in all in going forward. Stop worrying about quitting and get focused on doing what you are trained to do.

Every competitor has a moment where quitting may be the correct decision. There comes a time when what it takes to perform causes too much destruction, stealing from other areas of your life. Success requires so much of you that having to do it repeatedly can nearly destroy you. When and what are those thresholds?

I have found that the quit threshold rarely gets mentioned. How much you are willing to give is overlooked when you are mired in the misery of Suckville. Identifying that moment will not make you fail faster or have more struggles.

To break free from Suckville, you must identify your limits, and know the moment when you are willing to walk away from the competition. Anything short of that requires your total commitment.

That is why it is essential to change your quit moment. It is not about losing everything or staying too long, but it is not entertaining the constant barrage of quitting thoughts every single time it gets complicated. If you are in it for the long haul, stop thinking that you need to escape the pain. You can handle it.

Elite competitors do not fear failure and do not regret quitting. They only fear the moment when their efforts no longer result in success. That moment of absolute realization and clarity can be terrifying. But once you have quit, experienced failure, accepted your fate, there remains one thing to do next, and that is to get back to work. It is not the struggle that you have feared but realizing that your battle may result in quitting. It is mental 100% of the time.

You may have to quit. Everyone has that moment. But push your threshold back.

I doubt it is the right time. You have more to give.

Use Your Quit Moment as Momentum

I know you have had times that you wanted to quit and get away from the pains. You would be crazy not to feel that way. And yet, here you stand. You did not get beaten, and the struggle did not crush you. The game is still going on.

It is time to stop playing the victim. No one wants to hear how hard it has been anymore. It does not matter how much bad luck you have experienced. You are still in the competition, so it is time to fight back.

The fact you may decide to quit has consumed you. Who cares? Quitting, failure, and struggle are all part of success. Each is a significant risk to achieve greatness.

Are you competing to not struggle, or are you competing to achieve what you want?

If you can accept the consequences of failing, why are you trying to prevent it?

If you accept your life after your sport, why are you so worried about quitting?

Why are you wasting any energy on the "What If" world?

You can only choose one objective to focus on – success or preventing struggle. You cannot do both. You do not prevent a little bit of failure and you do not halfway succeed. There is never a combination of the two. It is either one or the other.

There is genius in your ability to work through problems. Your mind has fought against fears instead of working to escape Suckville because you have fixated on "not quitting."

The presence of difficulty does not have to be an invitation to quit.

Do not quit on yourself. Use that as momentum.

It reminds me of the fable - The Farmer's Donkey - that my dad used to share with me. I have never found who wrote it, but it is fitting to understand the value of mental flexibility in moments of crisis.

During a typical day on the farm, a farmer started hearing a horrible sound from off in the distance. It was so obnoxious that he had to investigate the source of the sound. As he began approaching the sound, it became more and more labored.

He found the source of the wailing – one of his oldest donkeys had fallen down an abandoned water well. When he peeked over the side, his donkey was near exhaustion from trying to climb out of the 8 foot deep well. He threw a rope down, but really, what was that going to do? It is not like the donkey would know what to do with a rope other than to pull on it. He tried to put a ladder down the hole, but have you ever seen a donkey try and climb a ladder? Every solution involved something the donkey had no idea what to do with it.

The final solution was to give up. The farmer decided to bury the donkey in the well. He called his friends and told them he needed their help. Each of his friends tried to give him another solution, but none made sense. He needed their help to bury the donkey. The inevitable was the only solution. As much as it pained him, he had to accept the outcome.

As he and his friends started shoveling dirt into the well, the donkey let out the worst screams. The donkey knew what was happening.

But then, as the donkey shook off the dirt, it stood upon the new bottom of the well. It was higher than it was 5 minutes ago. As additional dirt was added, the donkey kept standing taller. Eventually, the donkey was able to walk out of the well.

There will be times in your life that everything seems to be collapsing in all around you and your closest friends seem to be trying to bury you. But you can use your circumstances as the stepping stones to emerge from the depths of your struggles and start having success, even if people have given up on you. That is the moral of the Donkey in the Well story.

Find a way.

It would help if you adapted the way you think about Suckville.

A quit moment is on the table. So what?

There has always been a quit moment, but you MUST use the struggles to start building your way out of Suckville. By accepting there is an end, you are free to find a way forward.

Life provides you lessons every moment of the day. Some are easy, and some are painful. Your responsibility is to learn from the experiences of life. If you do not find the lessons, you will repeat the patterns and suffer much more difficult lessons until you face the learning in front of you. Separate yourself from the delivery of the message and listen for the pearls of the learning.

Suckville does not have to deliver the final nail in your coffin. You can decide when to walk away later. You will endure, and you will persevere. There is no evidence that your journey will defeat you.

Embrace the mental flexibility to adapt and grow through Suckville by reconnecting with your underlying processes and overall competitive genius. It is in there.

It is time to stop fearing failure, struggle, and quitting. All your worries have done nothing but created the exact misery that you have feared. The energy you have expended on your concerns has not worked to get you to where you want to be. It is time to put in place strategies designed to drive success. Fight for you from here forward.

Instead of obsessing about quitting, focus all your energies on taking care of the business in front of you. I want you prepared for the struggles that lie ahead, not be surprised by them. It is time to build your First Aid Kit for the dangers of your uncertain future.

First Aid Kits

You cannot go into the uncertainty of the future without the necessary tools to survive. If you were packing for an expedition, you would pack every single contingency possible. That would be smart.

Not enough competitors focus on the potential of struggle and have no intention of planning when to quit. That is why struggle and quitting have the power to take over your mind. You are not prepared for them.

What would it hurt to game plan for the worst-case scenario? It seems to me it would be excellent preparedness. Thinking about the worst-case scenario will not make it happen. My experience suggests that facing all the possibilities reduces the negative influence of the dangers.

Professional golfers are on an island during competition. They cannot communicate with their coaches and cannot call timeouts to slow the game down. While golf is not a fast sport, their minds move very fast in competition and go hyper-speed when mired in struggle, leading to destructive outcomes. The line between success and struggle is so fragile.

It had me thinking about how to prepare their minds for the uncertainty of competition. Most competitors have moments where their minds dream of flawless execution in the highest-pressure situations. The ideal performance becomes their standard, and expectations rise to unhealthy levels.

The heightened tension makes it impossible to play perfectly. Tension destroys rhythm and feel, critical for success in nearly every sport. As tension builds and the outcomes get more challenging, expectations rise to unhealthy levels. The combination of high risk and high expectations makes elite performance almost impossible.

This realization led me to create First Aid Kits for my professional golfers. The goal was to have three or four tangible and straightforward actions to take should trouble flood competition. When struggle clouds the mind, I do not want them searching for what to do. Instead, I want them to rely on a pre-determined action plan. Just like a First Aid Kit, you only need it when you need it.

A traditional First Aid Kit is a simple collection of the essential items needed to manage minor scrapes or respond to a significant emergency. It does not solve the problem that caused the crisis. Instead, it bridges the gap to get more comprehensive care. You never know when you need one, but you better be prepared just in case you do need one.

I encouraged my players to write down the three or four tangible items on an index card and keep them in their yardage book. I wanted the index card to be titled "In Case of Emergency" because when the competition gets chaotic, and you get mentally overwhelmed, it is hard to remember what to do. It would help if you had it easy, clear, and concise.

To build your First Aid Kit, start with a simple review of what you are the most confident doing when your mind gets overwhelmed with the chaos. I want you to think about times in the past when you have struggled, how did you push through and drive results. Those actions are essential to understand because you have confidence in the basic elements of your process. The core of your First Aid Kit starts with your most confident attributes.

The three most essential components of your emergency management plan form a stable mental structure. It is like a triangle, solid at the base and supporting both sides. Not one individual aspect of your kit is any more important than the other or comes in a particular order, but they support each other.

1. Acceptance

Acceptance is the most critical mental aspect of managing overwhelming struggles. There is a time to ask, "why is this happening?" and a time to ask, "what is the most important thing to do right now?" Too many competitors ask the wrong questions during a struggle. They get caught up in trying to understand why it suddenly got challenging. Difficulty does not invite the most rational thought.

Acceptance allows you to take in all the clutter without reacting too fast. Your First Aid Kit will enable you to know what is happening to you, not why the struggling is occurring.

Chasing the "WHY" in the heat of the moment will only distract you from pushing forward and emerging from the struggle. You can ask why it happened and what caused it to occur in your after-event analysis. But in the heat of the moment, you have to allow yourself the permission to be in the chaos and believe you can manage it.

Physical triggers or mental tricks can foster acceptance. The actual acts do not result in acceptance but are used in the chaos to direct your attention to higher acceptance. For instance, one of my professional players will re-tie his shoes when the game starts going sideways. The physical activity does not make him accept, but slowing down, taking the time to untie and then tie his shoes slows him down and allows him time to find the proper perspective.

I have a professional golfer who developed an elegant way to allow acceptance. I was watching him play in a tournament, and he started terribly. He was so angry that I was trying to find a way to sneak out of the tournament.

After the fifth hole, I saw him sitting on a cooler as he waited to tee off on a hole. He was eating a nutrition bar, slowly chewing the snack with his eyes closed. Because I could not speak with him at that moment, I had no idea what he was doing.

He birdied four of the next six holes. When he finished the round, we did a cursory review of his round. When things were going downhill for him, he decided to slow down and eat a snack.

The brilliance was that he tried to taste each ingredient in the bar. It reconnected him to the present moment and freed him up to play great golf.

Acceptance can also be grounded in your breath. Research has demonstrated time and time again the power of diaphragmatic, rhythmic, coordinated breathing exercises. I recommend all my athletes find the breathing regimen that they enjoy but start with Box Breathing.

Box Breathing is the practice of inhaling through your nose on a four-count, holding your breath for a four-count, and then exhaling through your mouth for an additional four count. Then repeat that process.

I like to use Box Breathing while imagining that I am running my hands through warm bathwater. It helps me feel the blood in my hands. Feeling that warmth reverses the feeling of the blood leaving my hands (that is precisely what is happening, by the way – study the Fight or Flight response for more information on the Sympathetic Hyperarousal). I like to do one additional modification during my exhale, which is I try to imagine that my belly button touches my spine. It is a trick I learned from a physical therapist after having surgery. When you imagine your belly button touching your spine, you fully release all of your remaining breath, completely relaxing.

The important thing about the different "tricks" is what they foster – acceptance. It is not the trick that did the job but the shift in mindset to accept what is happening and push forward with purposeful action.

2. Action

When I was pitching, I knew I had one pitch that I could always throw with confidence. It was a slider, a pitch I could throw hard, and I trusted my mechanics would work, even if I lost my feel on the mound. It took me a few years to learn and trust this pitch, but I found that it not only allowed me to trust one pitch, but it also seemed to always reconnect me to my mechanics for the rest of the inning. That slider became my safety blanket.

When it gets brutal, what can you trust?

Can you focus on playing great defense or lock down your opponent? Can you bring energy if that helps you?

You must have an action that you can trust. It should not take a ton of mental energy to execute. If you have to think about it, more than likely, it is not the right thing. Be careful not to overthink this Action step either. It is very rarely complicated, and often, it is so simple you overlook it.

To determine your trusted action step, consider the following:

- What do you like to rely on physically? What feels comfortable and confident?
- What result do you typically have when you trust this particular action?
- What gives you mental freedom so you can focus on working through the difficulty?

Every elite competitor will have a "go-to" action step when things get complicated. There may be a pass a quarterback likes to throw, a basketball player has a favorite side of the court to shoot from, and a soccer player has a favored leg to kick with when the game gets fast. Do not worry about your opponent knowing your secret because it is more critical for you to get through the mental swamp than your opponent out-smarting you.

3. Attitude

Emergency medical technicians undergo intense training to manage chaotic circumstances effectively. Significant attention gets paid to their mental processes under pressure to limit the extreme events' uncertainty, stress, and drama. According to a close professional colleague, the secret is an attitude of purpose, not apprehension.

"I have a job to do. I am not worrying about what will happen next."

Your attitude in the most challenging moments establishes your psychological flexibility. If you feel you are the reason for your struggles or need to transfer the blame, you are not using your attitude to persevere. You have to be prepared to focus differently.

Negative thoughts and judgmental assumptions will increase and attack your attitude. They will wear you down, resulting in a negative, defeatist attitude. To have Attitude on your First Aid Kit, you prepare for the most challenging aspects of chaos and how you can mentally engage in those moments.

"You can handle anything so long as you face it."

"You are ready to meet the challenge."

Those seem like very benign statements, but they are very constructive and supportive. The pronoun matters - YOU!

I have found that athletes that use the YOU modifier have better engagement because "I" can sometimes feel judgmental or pressure-inducing. Give it a shot when things get difficult in training and see if using YOU helps you overcome your challenges.

Having something in case of emergency should free up your mind from worrying about the potential of trouble. You would not jump out of an airplane without a parachute, and you probably would not trust someone else to pack your parachute. Confidence in managing an uncertain future requires you to have something concrete and actionable you can trust.

The creation of your First Aid Kit also allows you to become more vulnerable to the uncertainty of competition. Knowing you have the necessary tools to meet the potential of any future challenges pulls you out of dread and into determination. That is powerful.

The last aspect of a First Aid Kit that is important to consider is having one in general. It is not a fix.

A First Aid Kit keeps you focused in the present moment. When you have a plan for the chaos, everything slows down.

If you are prepared for the difficult, delay quitting. When things intensify, you are getting closer to your goal.

Go down memory lane to your favorite movies for a minute.

Did Luke Skywalker have resistance the closer he got to The Death Star?

Did Indiana Jones have it easier the closer he got to The Temple of Doom?

Did the Cleveland Indians and Charlie Sheen win the American League Pennant in Major League without defeating the New York Yankees? Exactly my point.

16

GAIN GREATER WISDOM

Your experiences have value in your future. Each disappointment creates the catalyst to prepare you for the opportunities in your life. It is up to you to understand the value instead of allowing yourself to get caught up in the drama.

When I was in clinical training, I would spend hours learning every aspect of clinical diagnostics because I never wanted to miss anything. It was essential to know each condition's nuances to understand the intricate differences driving a patient's suffering. I would make notecards, watch videos of case studies, and read anything I could related to diagnosis and treatment, but it did not help me become a better psychologist. I lacked experience.

I became a psychologist because of my struggles as an athlete. I always struggled to find the extra mental gear in competition. I would do what it took, to the letter of the law, but never seemed to get over the hump. It was not until I completely lost it, became a full-time resident of Suckville did I find my pathway through my continual struggles. It was the best thing to happen to me.

It was not until a psychologist mentored me that I gained an understanding of my perspective. It was not about what I learned in the books. My success was about 85% of the application of the knowledge.

Magic happens when you use that 85% and then permit yourself to trust the remaining 15% of your intuition, experiences, and gut instincts to take it the rest of the way. My mentor would quiz me over and over again, ranging from diagnosis to treatment and case management. Nothing was by the book.

"Your clinical skills become the combination of your knowledge, personal experiences, and professional history. What is important is your ability to trust your impressions. That is wisdom."

That was the best advice I received from my mentor. It has stayed with me ever since. It was not just about what I knew but how my experiences shaped my impressions. With each experience, my perspective grew.

The best become wise in their growth.

In the middle of a struggle, you will not see the wisdom that is crystalizing. But it is happening inside you. You must trust the process.

Struggle creates such mental clutter that you do not see the depth of the work underneath the surface.

Just like you do not see the seeds growing under the soil, your wisdom builds away from your awareness. It must because if you could see your understanding growing, you would never let it happen.

You are impatient by design. It is not natural to be patient. It is not human to simply wait for good things to come your way. The mental search for more and better can be helpful, but it can be dangerous. It is up to you to balance it.

While impatience can inspire you to ask for better, it can short-circuit growth. Some things need time. Others require you to demand better.

I have no shortcuts to gaining wisdom. It takes experience, time, and knowledge. Once it sets in and is allowed to grow, it is genius. To foster the development of wisdom, you must have some aspects in place – an organized mind, a desire to learn, and a way to record progress. To me, that is it. Wisdom is growth with scars. It is culture and passion. It is immeasurable, but you know it when you have it.

An Organized Mind

Life would be easy if it followed the grand plan, that process you thought would happen from the outset. But it never does. Things will change, others will challenge you, and some will downright threaten to break you.

Your mind is like the windshield of your car. It is hard to drive fast, respond to the road curves, and manage the distractions if you cannot see what is in front of you. You must be mentally organized to meet each demand you face.

Spending time to get your mind organized before competition can become a game-changer.

Most athletes train to fix the problems they are experiencing. When I start with a new professional client, they usually are very motivated to get started. It is common to have a list of factors to address. Once you correct a few uncomfortable aspects, it opens the door for me to go deeper mentally. I almost always focus on mental organization.

Mental organization is like cleaning closets. You must declutter, removing the clothes you no longer wear and get rid of the out-of-date fashions. It requires some hard questions, but they are necessary to free-up the mind to perform optimally.

An organized mind is the foundation for wisdom. Clutter does nothing but rob energy from the growth process. You often hold on to the chaos because that makes you feel like you are doing something. It may not be beneficial, but you are doing something. You must resist the urge to do something just because it is an activity.

To start organizing your mind:

1. Take a Personal Inventory

Who are you?

Serious question. Are you who you want to be?

Who you project to be and who you are can be two very different realities. It is essential to strip away the façade you have been living and start learning who you are. It will be scary. Trust me.

What do you want in your life?

What do you want people to say about you when you leave the room?

How do people feel when you interact with them?

A personal inventory is more about listening than anything else. The authentic you is deep inside but gets covered by the societal demands and false narratives you think you need to succeed. That is all wrong – LEARN TO BE YOU! As long as you are not doing anything to harm another, I need you to be you.

My true self was covered up because I wanted to be respected, trusted, and liked. I was a "people pleaser." I wanted to be valued, so instead of being me, I tried to be what I thought others wanted me to be. I was exhausted.

I was terrified of letting people down and getting upset or disappointed with me. As a result, instead of giving them my best, I gave them what I thought they wanted. And they were still unhappy. I was trying to figure them out, and in the process, I lost who I was.

It was not until I started studying myself did I feel connected. I organized my mind, and I emerged a different, more confident person. I emerged from the shadows. It was terrifying but necessary, vulnerable, and powerful.

You must know who you are.

You are not broken and do not have to change the core of who you are.

I want you to grow. I want you to be you.

Sit in silence and start writing, journaling, and thinking. I want you to open up your soul – the human side, the performance side, and the competitor side. They can all co-exist. But you have to listen to who you are – the desires and the fears. Both are there.

Stop being what others say you should be. I do not care what others post on social media. If you want to carry their baggage, then you can live their lives. Until then, live you.

Taking an inventory of you is nothing more than starting to listen, observe, and experience the full you. It is time to reintroduce you to you. Formal therapy can help, but so can the simple acts of prayer, sitting in silence, or active reflection. Start there.

2. Determine Your Direction

The following question is an important issue that often gets misunderstood.

What direction are you going in your life?

You are either moving in a powerful direction or stuck stagnate, paralyzed by life. There is no gray area. When I hear people say they are stuck, it is not that they are stagnating; it is just that they are moving too slow or lack a direction, nearly going in circles.

Are you moving towards what you want to accomplish or running away from your fears?

If you are running from struggle, afraid of the fears becoming a reality, you will be motivated by pain relief. It is no longer about feeling success as much as it is escaping the pains. Your direction becomes your navigational course.

If you do not know where you are going, you will never know if you arrive at your destination. The lack of an organized mind guarantees your endless search for comfort, relief, and confusion with where your feet are. To be mentally organized, you have to know what direction you are going.

Often, the pure existence of struggle motivates you to change course, to make a drastic course correction. Resist that urge. Keep your direction moving towards your desires, and do not let up. Your approach has to be clear to be organized. The friction you are experiencing is not forcing you to change. Instead, see the struggles as reminders to reconnect to your direction.

3. Make It Yours

Why do you do things the way you do them?

"It is the way I have always done it!"

"I was taught to do it this way."

"Because I just do."

These explanations are some of the greatest threats to success.

You are the guru of your life and performance. Believe it or not, you know how to build your plan for improvements.

I am not suggesting that you abandon the successful processes of the world's best. Absolutely not, but you need to learn from the best and incorporate it into your language to become yours.

If you could build your processes to drive your success the way you want it, what would you do?

Do not get stuck in the conventional method of thinking.

You do not have to workout at 5 am to get a good training session completed. It is not a sign of mental toughness compared to working out at night. Just get the workout in.

You do not have to have just one coach. Build the influencers in your life the way you want them. Build your agenda, process, and approach to make your psychological fingerprint.

Building Wisdom

Wisdom builds when you take learnings from many different sources and meld them into your experiences. Steve Jobs built Apple by trusting his instincts and building products that he would personally want. He did not rely on marketing and consumer focus groups.

Too many defer to the opinions of outsiders instead of trusting what they know. I have watched professional athletes who have won more in highly tense competitions defer to coaches that promise state-of-the-art training solely based on theory, only to get frustrated when the application falls short. You cannot replicate the "heat of the moment" experience.

Now, that does not mean there is not a place for outsiders. Absolutely there is. Many coaches are brilliant developers of talent, strategists, and leaders who had limited competitive success as a player or did not even play at all. What makes them great is that they understand how to communicate to bridge that gap. They make it about the player and how the player can incorporate that level of information.

It is like dancing. If I taught you all the correct moves, you would know the dance steps. But when the music comes on, I want to feel the music and make it yours. Do not dance like a robot, being 100% perfect with the steps but looking robotic. I watch players try so hard to do it "right" instead of making it their own.

Your mind works the way your mind works. It is truly personal to you. Make it yours and then own it.

1. Find the Simple First

To be organized, keep it simple. It is not any more complicated than that. There is beauty in simplicity.

Because you can does not mean you should.

That goes for simplicity. Learn to see the simple path forward and develop the most significant impact with the fewest resources needed to accomplish the task.

I call it the Cheeseburger Test.

When I go to a restaurant, I often order a cheeseburger. While I love them, there is a deeper reason behind this approach.

If the kitchen can prepare a cheeseburger the correct way, show attention to detail, and use great ingredients, I know they are willing to focus on the little things to be successful. Although I am not a chef and never worked in a professional kitchen, a cheeseburger is not a complicated item to produce with consistency. But too many restaurants take too many shortcuts. They use frozen, mass-produced beef patties and throw condiments on the plate. If they want to hide their lack of focus, they slather the cheeseburger with barbeque sauce or other sloppy disguises.

Great restaurants produce great burgers. They use the best ingredients and hand-pack the patties. The lettuce, tomato, and pickles are fresh, and the buns accentuate the flavor profile. It does not cost much money, but it does take elevated attention to detail.

If you cannot make a good burger and it is on your menu, why would I trust you to pay attention to other details? A great burger is straightforward, but that is the trap.

2. Stay Simple to Stay Organized

An organized mind is an invitation to build the long-term success you want because you can respond to challenges more efficiently. The mental energy does not deplete other resources, allowing you to multitask, manage multiple demands, and perform at your best.

A few factors cause disorganization – stress, fear, boredom, and lack of focus. Each is a threat, even though it may take time to create the destruction. It is hard to resist the threats and stay organized mentally when these are present.

Stress is one of the most destructive forces in your world. You can try to manage it, but it is always there. Stress is any internal or external demand that requires you to respond, either by enduring, resisting, or responding to the issue. It is not necessarily a bad thing, but the minor stressful demands can snowball to impede progress over time. Of course, major stressors can derail you in an instant.

The critical thing to realize about stress is that you are using energy to manage its impact. You can only ignore it for so long, so the continual response results in losing essential resources for more important factors. I have worked with athletes who struggle to keep their stress from invading them on the competitive field and get frustrated by their impaired performance. Eventually, stress invades their mind.

Fear is related to stress, but it is a much larger worry and will cause you to do what it takes to avoid the fears. If you are worried about something, your mind abandons its organization and directs all its attention to protect you against the fears and threats. That works if it is a clearly defined threat.

Fear often bleeds into many different threats, creating danger in relatively everyday experiences. The "What If" is too important to ignore and disrupts mental organization by taking over mental resources.

At the moment, your mind is focused, but the results get left in total disarray. It is what is left behind that is the most disruptive.

Boredom is a real threat to competitors. I have found that those who have had success always lose the spark at some point. At the outset, the novelty and challenge are inspiring, but over time, the journey can get very dull. There are only so many challenges and different ways to fight.

When you get bored, your mind loses the focus and organization in favor of the newer, shinier challenge. If you find yourself bored, you have to reconnect to particular challenges within the journey. Focus on the steps, not the staircase.

Finally, related to boredom is the lack of focus. As a competitor, the more success you achieve, the greater the number of opportunities that arise. I have worked with athletes who must carve out training time with limited availability because of distractions with business meetings or media obligations. It is part of the success process but causes risks in your mind. Every fruit eventually spoils, and the new opportunities constantly distract from the core tasks at hand.

Your mind functions best when it is clear and focused. When your mind gets connected to the process, wisdom grows. Learn to organize your mind because you are the only one who suffers when it is not organized.

3. Be a Lifelong Learner

You are never too old to learn something new. Wisdom is a constant hunger that must be fed. It is your responsibility to keep learning to enhance your experiences.

I have witnessed too many successful individuals resist new experiences because they are afraid to admit they do not have all the answers. As my mother told me long ago, "an expert is the one who asks. The idiot is the one who thinks people should ask them."

True statement.

While I recommended you know who you are and trust your instincts earlier, it is crucial to be willing to learn as much as you can. There are so many great teachers in your world, but you must be open to the lessons. If you close your mind, you shut down the opportunity to grow.

You will have more than one mentor in your life. You will learn more than one way to succeed before you create your path.

You must experiment and test new theories as you refine your approach. Innovation always starts with the way you think, so allow the sparks to fuel your passion. Learn from others, read books, listen to lectures, and observe as much as you. Do not stay confined to your area either.

I want all my athletes and coaches to learn from the most successful competitors in other sports. Just because they do not play your sport does not mean that you cannot learn something from them. I encourage all my coaches to spend time in their athletic departments with the coaches from other sports. I want my college coaches to find experts on their campuses from a variety of different topics. You do not have to reach out to the national experts when the best may be in your local area and willing to help.

At the end of your life, your experiences will look like a bookshelf. Will it be organized, diverse, and developmental?

I hope so.

4. Review Your Performance

The further you go, the more you are at risk to lose. Risk is the responsibility of success. It is why you may struggle with the fear of success - it brings a more significant impact of failure.

But it also brings perspective.

If you do not write down your learnings and experiences, how long do you think you will remember your experiences?

Will you remember what matters or only what you want to recognize?

Let me share one major performance secret – journaling is the most important psychological task you can do. All my clients are encouraged to journal their training, experiences, and daily progress. When they stop journaling, I have found that they begin to struggle again.

Unfortunately, they rarely see the relationship between their journaling and their performance. Taking the time to record the data and details refocuses the mind and organizes the experiences, fostering an environment for wisdom.

My prompts for journaling are relatively straightforward. Each of these prompts are part of the journal that I developed called *The Elite Journal.* They are:

1. Write down three things you did well today.
2. Write down three things you struggled with today.
3. Write down three things you learned today.

Do this every day.

Go into the details. In the *Elite Journal*, the prompts go deeper into your experience, including the thoughts, fears, and doubts present in pressure situations. Details are where your lessons live.

Take 15 minutes each evening to contribute to your journal. Do not cut this short. It is as important as doing your physical training each day.

At the beginning of every month, I want you to go back and read your past month. That is it. Nothing more.

Journaling makes you think, write, and then read the material, so you are essentially getting three reviews of the experience each day. It helps you also get the worries and stresses of your mind down on paper, out of your head where you cannot do anything about them. I like seeing concrete tasks versus obsessing about the ones in my head.

What Sucks Is Your Support

Every experience has led you to something better in the future. It may not result in a different outcome, but your process may improve or become more efficient in the execution. It does not always mean more success tangibly, but wisdom grew if you chose to accept it.

You cannot immediately leave Suckville. One magical performance will not spark a return of all your confidence that has been absent. It always takes time to leave Suckville in your past.

Why would you want to lose all the powerful lessons associated with being in Suckville? The struggles have contributed to who you are today and who you will be in the future. There is tremendous value in that.

Jerry White is an international conflict resolution specialist awarded the Nobel Prize for Peace in 1997 as part of The International Campaign to Ban Landmines organization. While on a college trip to Jerusalem, White lost his leg in a landmine explosion. The devastating experience for a young adult male shifted his life in a way that has positively impacted millions, even if they do not know him by name. I didn't.

About fifteen years ago, I organized a personal development seminar. I wanted a national speaker and bestselling author to headline the event, but the speaking agent recommended White as a package deal. All the agent said was that he one of the most dynamic speakers on their list. When the agent added that he was a close friend to the late Princess Diana, I had to take the risk.

The agent was not wrong.

While the national speaker was a total disaster, White was the best speaker I had ever heard. White captivated the audience with his humility, struggles, and his recovery that was the catalyst for his life.

We went to dinner, and I was mesmerized. White shared the story of losing his leg and dealing with the unbelievable pain when he was so far from home. While hospitalized, he learned to listen to the stories of the other patients who also lost their limbs from undiscovered, left-behind landmines from past wars.

When White left the hospital, he rebuilt his life. While he was not lost, but he did not have the direction he desired.

A phone call changed when a colleague asked him if he would be interested in getting rid of landmines from war-torn countries. His work led him to Princess Diana, and they formed a deep friendship. They traveled the world together as she put her own life back together. They wanted to make the world better and reconnected to their purposes in life.

I have stayed in touch with White, and he continues to inspire me. He has worked and consulted with governments, corporations, and entities across the globe. His most powerful recommendation was – "do not see your struggles, your pains, and your past as disabilities. Instead, see them as reminders to bring peace forward."

White wants the world to know that life will knock you down, but instead of feeling like a victim, become the victor. The only way to do that is to face each challenge head-on and use your experiences as the spark to solve the challenges you have.

When he spoke to our audience, White told a story of walking the streets of Cambodia when he came across a young girl. This young girl worked so hard to make sure all the other street children were getting their food, taking charge of the group. White was struck, not by her work, but that she was doing all the work with an amputated lower left leg. With every stumble, she would get back up and keep going. She was never discouraged.

When she noticed White, she pointed to his leg, as if saying, "you are missing your leg too?" He said he nodded yes, then sat down and took off his leg. She smiled at him and went back to work. He put his leg back on and got to work too. It was not about their disabilities but their abilities. He did not feel sorry for himself, and she did not feel sorry for herself. They were too busy.

Stop feeling sorry for yourself. The struggle will end, and you will be better for it. It may be the best thing to ever happen to you, but it will continue to disable you if you wallow in the misery. Suckville happens, but it does not have to define you.

My dad became physically disabled in his early 60's. Without much warning, he lost the feeling below both of his knees, making it hard to balance and walk. He had every medical diagnostic work-up possible, and the diagnosis remained unknown. He wore prosthetics from his knees down to continue walking, stabilizing his feet, and allowing him to stand. He wore them everywhere.

When my family went to Disney World, I wanted to rent my father an electric scooter to get around the parks. He refused. The only way he would go to the parks with his grandchildren was to walk the parks and stand in line like everyone else, probably 10 miles per day for a week.

He hated his prosthetics. They were a symbol of his disability and loss of function. As a former collegiate athlete and proud military man, my dad's physical stature was a source of pride. He was also a pharmacist and would stand for twelve-hour shifts. While he never let his disability slow him down, I know that he hated the effort it took to simply live somewhat normal.

But his disability saved his life.

Approximately two years before his death, he had a complex surgery. A few days after the surgery, he crashed medically.

The medical team had one choice – a life-saving surgery with a low chance of success. We had no choice. We knew survival meant additional disability, but living was more important than dying.

During the surgery, the surgeon gave us an update. "He is doing far better than anticipated. His heart is like an 18-year-old marathon runner. It is the reason he is going to survive."

The things he hated more than anything else – his prosthetics – saved his life. With every labored step he took for eight years, he was strengthening the conditioning of his heart.

He had no idea why, but those prosthetics prepared him for the most significant challenge in his life. Because he survived the risky surgery, we spent two quality years with my dad, which were truly invaluable.

Those two additional years were a gift. Everyday became a blessing and it allowed each of us to truly live purposefully with dad.

What you hate right now will make you the strongest you have ever been. Those challenges will help you face each challenge in your life.

Trust me. Suckville does not suck. Suckville makes you better.

17

WHAT ARE YOU CAPABLE OF?

You have lived your life constrained by the potential of risk, never by the potential of possibilities. There is nothing wrong with that approach, but it has not prepared you for what you are doing right now. Competition is always messy and never according to a plan. The game is unpredictable and challenging, but you achieve much more than your fears.

Your true power lies in your ability to get into the unknown and thrive. If you focus on the strange things, those aspects of your competition and psyche that you have never experienced, you will be terrified. That is natural. Despite all the uncertainty and chaos of competition lies the only constant – YOU!

You need to see yourself winning championships, breaking through the challenges, and walking out of the arena as a champion. If you cannot visualize yourself succeeding, then you will see yourself struggling. Your mind must grasp one side of that scenario.

You are what and how you think you are. More importantly, you fear what you fear you are.

Who Determines Your Value?

No one on the outside can define your value as a competitor. Your coach, a stat line, or the number of victories is nothing more than external influences. Some are positive and some are negative, but none have the right to define your worth.

Despite your successes or struggles, your value transcends any outcome, status, or level of performance. Your value is how you face challenges, what you learn from those struggles, and how you treat others. That does not require any talent or skill set to do effectively.

The media loves to glorify every transgression among athletes but rarely highlights the human side of elite athletes. It is a shame because I have witnessed amazing interactions of my athletes, far away from the limelight or media attention. They wanted it like that.

There is one memory that I hold fondly of one of my professional clients. This professional athlete had achieved immeasurable success early in his career. Many would consider him to be stand-offish, arrogant, and even self-centered. That was honestly my impression when I was brought on his team as well.

Yet, there he stood with a young family. A mother, a father, a brother, and a young girl with a noticeable medical condition were locked into a deep conversation with my player. They were not aware that he was struggling so profoundly that he had started to hate the game. He was a shell of his former self and was lost in his mental struggles.

This family did not care how he was doing right now. They were mesmerized with the man, not the athlete.

I watched the conversation for 45 minutes. It was genuine and authentic. Both sides were laughing, at times wiping away tears, and other times hugging. They finished with a prayer and hugged again. As the family left, the player just watched them disappear into the darkness of the parking lot. It was a powerful moment for the player.

In the short time that I had worked with this player, I had come to respect him so much. He was kind, genuine, and had a breath of vulnerability that many on the outside perceived as being conceited. His emotions were on his sleeve every single day, sometimes to his detriment. The game sometimes loved him back, but it was often a contentious relationship.

When he returned to where I was sitting, I asked him who they were. He said he did not know them until they had messaged him on social media and wanted to meet. Their daughter loved to watch him play and asked for a chance to take a picture. He gave them so much more than that.

He asked me a poignant question after that. "Doc, why do I forget the platform I have when I find myself fighting the game? I started in this game because I loved the challenge. Every morning, I would look forward to the game, to playing with friends, and doing this for a living. I watched my heroes play and looked up to them so much. Now, I am in their position and find myself out of energy so often. My value has become my level of play. Then I have a meeting like this, so why does it make me feel guilty?"

Honestly, how am I supposed to answer a question that deep?

He was correct that he was allowing his level of play to influence his perspective. While it is normal and has probably happened to you, you can slow your approach and pivot to a healthier mindset.

I challenged him to see things differently and view his emotional energy as a treasured resource. Everyone only has so much energy to give during a day, and everything you do takes energy away from you. If you deplete your energy on unnecessary things, you will not have any left when you need it.

I challenged him to view his mental energy like a jar of pennies. One hundred pennies, to be exact.

Every morning, I told him, he wakes up with one hundred pennies in a jar. Everything he does in the day, every mental worry, every competition, and even relaxing, takes some pennies out of the jar. The number of pennies it takes from the jar is wholly dependent upon how much energy the challenge requires. Further, his emotional frustrations, worries, and anger also take pennies from his jar. Everything takes at least one penny, but the more angst he feels means it requires more pennies.

When he sits down with his children and wife at the end of the day, how many pennies will he have left?

That is truly up to where he spends his energy during the day.

How many pennies does he want to spend…

- On training for competition?
- On competing?
- On dealing with trolls on social media?
- On obsessing about the future performances?

- On responding to critics?
- On proving doubters wrong?
- On showing his colleagues how good he is?
- On his frustrations on his lack of progress?
- On his image among the greats in the game?

You get my point. The question challenged the player.

When he showed up the next day, he had a penny in his hand. He told me that he thought long and hard about his past year's performances and realized that he was giving everything away to things beyond his control. When he got home, he had nothing left for his family. It angered him. He had lost himself in distractions beyond his control.

He carried that penny in his pocket. When he found himself getting angry, frustrated, or worried, he would hold the penny and ask himself, "Is this truly worth my last penny?"

The answer was always no.

Where are you giving up your value?

As you have struggled to find joy in the game again, I want you to reconnect to where you give your energy. Your value will be determined by how you leave the world, and I want you to leave it better than you found it.

Every person you meet will be better because you were present with them. You will be better because instead of seeing your place in Suckville as your legacy, you are going to change it, face it, and dominate it.

You hold that penny. It is your choice how you see things going forward. Choose to focus on the things that matter.

18

IT IS TIME TO BREAK FREE

In preparing to write this book, I spent quite a bit of time reflecting on my life. I have learned from great mentors over the years from a variety of different backgrounds. Those men and women hold so much wisdom about navigating the trials and tribulations of life and have such powerful perspectives gained by their own experiences. I trust that each person came into my life for a reason, and I hope I learned everything I could from them.

Life is a classroom. Your experiences have prepared you for something you will encounter later. It is hard to understand what your future holds, but you must believe you are ready for any challenge you will face.

Suckville does not need to be a terrible experience. When you are in the middle of it, there is no doubt the pain of misery can reach intolerable levels. Yet, you have found a way to continue forward to the point you are at today.

I have consoled players struggling with the harsh decision to retire and helped them manage the immense pressures in their lives. I have helped make sense of the mysterious nature of their struggles and then watched them become All-Americans by merely shifting their perspective.

I watched athletes terrified of the unknown work hard to find a personal reset and break free from their struggles. Those same players have become leaders, captains, and record holders, using those struggles to enhance their character.

I had players write their retirement speech, only to burn it when they signed a large contract extension. The simple act of accepting the end gave them a new beginning.

In each scenario, the common factor was their willingness to see their personal place in Suckville as a learning laboratory versus the final epithet. It was never easy for them and will not be easy for you.

Learning requires frustration and confusion. The greatest lessons in your life have been the most challenging moments, which triggered the greatest insecurities and most painful doubts. Yet, you worked to clear the confusion and found the lesson through the clutter.

If everything were easy, you would never fight to succeed. Your perseverance grows through each fight. What you once thought would knock you down is nothing but a slight distraction today. Learning cannot grow into wisdom unless there is a painful fight associated with it.

You simply must keep pushing forward, one small effort at a time. I do not know the timeline you are on, but no one will come and make it easier for you. You do not need it either. True wisdom emerges from Suckville when YOU find the elements of your process in the most significant periods of darkness. In your worst moments, you will find the light for your path.

Who knows when you will reach your summit of success? You must make every day the most successful it can be by devoting all your energy to the purpose in front of you. That is all you can do.

Success is like advancing in a video game. When you first start, the challenges appear simple. The purpose is to learn the basic skills necessary to succeed at the game. With each level you complete, the challenges get more complicated.

It may take multiple attempts to complete the level, and you probably get frustrated having to start at the beginning of each level after failing to advance. You do it time and time again (if you do not use a cheat code!).

Eventually, you learn how to win the level and advance in the game. With new levels come new challenges, just like life. The more success you have, the more complex the challenges become. The goal is to learn from each challenge and grow forward.

Moment by moment, you start advancing by focusing your mind on what you can control and learn from what you cannot. There is power in being okay with where you are and building forward despite the challenges, which are nothing more than opportunities to learn and grow. Success does not have a specific plan, and there are no cheat codes. You must keep working on it.

The most important question you can ask yourself is, "What can I rely on to face the unknown before me?" Knowing the most impactful answer is YOU, then you are free to work through every circumstance and challenge. Just do not ever give up.

You do not have to be confident to push forward or to identify a specific goal. You do not need to eat steel, sit in freezing water, or meditate like a Tibetan monk to prove you are mentally ready. You simply must be willing to walk into the uncertainty in front of you.

Breaking free from Suckville comes down to your choice – do you take the easy path or the unchartered one?

The easy way is to stop giving your all and to look for a quick fix. Because you want to avoid discomfort, you do not care about the lost learnings and experiences.

The rugged, unchartered path is precisely that – unknown. You must be willing to venture into the darkness and believe in yourself to persevere.

No one has the same conditions as you, and no one has your psychological fingerprint. This journey and your response are unique to you. The challenges are problematic because they are personal. Learning to face uncertainty with your skill sets and mentality will help you succeed with future challenges.

You have been challenged to be in the position you are in today by a variety of forces. None have been presented to you because you are weak—quite the opposite. You are at this point in your life because you are strong and have the potential to be impressive.

Do not allow your struggle to become your standard because you latched on to the mythical "potential" instead of learning to accept how you are. Your potential will always be out of reach, so start making your reality better every day. It is time to stop hanging on to the illusion of your potential and start accepting who you are. You are in the right place right now, for you.

It is time to change your mindset and embrace the exact moment you are in now. Look at what you can do and how you will progress through the uncertainty in your future. Along the way, you must learn every single lesson presented to you, and only then will you see the reasons for your lessons.

Once you determine that Suckville has no power over you, you grow. It is not your eternity. You will stay in Suckville forever.

Accept who you are and how magnificent that is. Work every day to learn more about yourself and gain more wisdom.

It is now your time to break free of the mental chains you have used to limit your growth and start using them to climb into your future. It is time to realize your reality is damn impressive and only going to get better.

There are five things you can do every day to have great success. If you focus on these, you will no longer feel stuck, and they will individually create an impactful day.

1. Show Up

It may be hard to show up when days are challenging, but avoiding the challenge makes it worse. Show up with what you have and try and get better. Get better every day. You do not need to be perfect to be successful. Just be you.

2. Stand Up

Be prepared for anything and expect nothing from the game or life. Be confident in who you are and believe you can endure anything. You can dominate any challenge if you give all of who you are for the entire challenge. Stop worrying about what could happen and stand up to everything that does happen. You can handle it.

3. Face the Challenge

Accept the responsibilities of the challenge before you, and do not look to transfer blame and responsibility. Work through each level and keep fighting. Nothing will destroy you. Work through each challenge with a relentless attitude and do not give up.

4. Make Someone's Life Better

The greatest gift you have is the ability to improve the life of another. Share your wisdom with others. You will learn perspective and purpose through your giving. Whenever you feel lost, give guidance to others on their journey. Your experiences may be a source of valuable wisdom for someone else and you will learn from this experience too.

5. Leave It Better Than You Found It

Leaving a powerful legacy requires you to leave things better than you found them. Clean up the messes around you, so others do not get caught up in your leftovers. Focus on your legacy, through the good times and bad, as that will persist much longer than wins and losses or any performance statistics.

Time to Make the Mental Changes

Your time in Suckville will make you better in the long run. The positive and negative experiences simply prepare you for future challenges. What matters is that you are ready for what the future holds.

You did not find yourself in Suckville because you were mentally weak or a bad person. Struggle follows all competitors, and it will eventually take over if you are not careful. The game will eventually become a burden. I have met very few competitors who have been able to avoid the pains of Suckville.

Through it all, you have become stronger, mentally and physically. Do not see the future as being fearful, but instead see yourself capable to handle anything that may happen. You can face anything if you believe in your ability to endure the challenges and use your mental flexibility to work your way through the difficulties.

Your circumstances are what they are, neither positive or negative, just events waiting for you to label them as good or bad. You have certain things in your life and game that may make success more difficult, but that does not mean you cannot succeed. What matters is what you are willing to endure to push through. Use the circumstances, challenges, and barriers to reinforce your process and determination. You will not break, and you are not alone.

If you could surround yourself with supporters who had a positive heart and mindset, you would soar. Unfortunately, when you are struggling, you lose that focus and get attracted to the naysayers and discontents. You must prioritize building a supportive environment to be successful. It is extremely difficult to succeed within a toxic culture.

You must break free from those who do not want you to succeed. Your competitors may be terrified of success or intimated by yours, but you are not responsible for their misery. Look at the people in your life and figure out who is there for you and who is making it harder on you.

The people in your life are energy transmitters. They will either build or destroy your energy. If you are sitting with someone anxious and worried, you will sense their energy. On the flip side, if you are around someone with that positive perspective and are excited about the future, you can feel that. You will continue to attract what you think, so you must protect yourself against negative people.

You are playing your own game. If you do not like your rules, change them. Success is never guaranteed, and your timeline may not seem fast enough, but you are worth your investment. Stay with your progress and start focusing on the little choices that lead to your decisions. Your momentum will grow through the smaller efforts. Win the little moments!

If you change your perspective, you will begin to see opportunities instead of disappointments.

It only takes a small shift in your thinking to see what is possible. Your doubts, insecurities, and negative thoughts are nothing more than noise. Focus on what you can do and do not let up.

Refine your process while you emerge from Suckville. Focus on your continual improvement and search for more effective and efficient ways to succeed. While there are no shortcuts, there are better ways to do things. Find those!

Do not be afraid to change your environment. You do not owe anyone anything. If someone is not a positive influence, protect yourself from their negativity. All it takes is one person to pee in the pool to ruin it for everyone. Do not let anyone pee in your pool.

Finally, do not quit. You are worth your efforts. All your work will pay off in the future. Who knows what it will look like, but you will know it when you experience it. Success is funny, just like confidence. Many times, you do not realize it when you have it, only when it leaves you. Focus on what you can do, and everything will take care of itself.

The mental changes will create a more successful future. To make them more impactful, here are five additional thoughts to make success last for you:

1. Honor Those Before You and Respect Where You Are

I want you to have respect for the challenges and difficulty of what you are trying to do. It is more than going through the motions or just trying to make it to the next day. Learn about your journey, those who came before you, and those who will follow you. It will not add pressure. It will emphasize perspective.

What you are doing is not easy, so it is valuable to see the complete picture of where you are, what you are trying to accomplish and respect the challenge.

There are many who have walked before you. Learn from their lessons and study their successes and failures. Honor their contributions to where you are today. If you play in a large stadium and have the coolest gear in the country, I can guarantee there were players playing on that exact same field, with substandard facilities, and cheap uniforms. They built the foundation so you can reach the next level. Honor those who came before you.

2. Expect Nothing From Others

No one is going to make it happen for you. That does not mean that no one will help you. Instead, no one will solve your struggles for you. I have found that players stuck in Suckville often get frustrated with coaches and teammates for not helping them in their struggle more. Expect nothing from anyone. Take care of your own business.

You do not need someone to remind you to do extra work or focus on the most important things. There is no one outside of you who can make that happen. It has to come from you.

When you expect nothing from others, you are never let down. If you want to perform better, start working towards improvements. It is up to you.

A coach will not give you more opportunities, and the outside influences or voices will not quiet down, no matter how much you want them to. If you do not like your level of performance, it is up to you to improve as much as you can to change your environment. The more you beg for attention, the less you get.

3. Anticipate the Difficulties

When you are struggling, it is hard to anticipate that additional difficulties will continue. Your mind wants to project the easy path, resulting in astronomical expectations and keeping you frustrated.

If you have ever been on an airplane and experienced air turbulence, you know about anticipating difficulties. I was on a flight a few years ago and went through some brutal turbulence. The flight crew did not say anything before the turbulence started and never said how long it would last. The hour of bumps was not fun. I was sweating and stressed out.

A few months later, I was on a cross-country flight that had a much different experience. Prior to take off, the pilot announced that the flight would encounter turbulence about an hour prior to landing, but that he would do everything he could to make it comfortable for the passengers. Four hours into the flight, the pilot announced that the turbulence would start in thirty minutes, so he encouraged passengers to go to the bathroom, stow their laptops, and buckle their seatbelts. He counted down every ten minutes, then five minutes, and then announced a two-minute warning.

I was ready. I am not a fan of turbulence, not because it makes me feel bad. I do not like seeing others get airsick, so I would prefer if flights were smooth. When the bumps started, they only lasted one minute and then it was over. That was it!

Upon landing, the pilot explained that pilots from other flights had reported on unpredictable turbulence, so he felt it was important to prepare the entire flight for the possibility instead of being surprised. He said that in his twenty years of flying, he has learned that prepared passengers are happy passengers.

He was right. I was not happy with the pilot of the flight who did not announce the turbulence or give any timeframe for its duration. I was prepared for much worse on the cross-country flight and was happy the turbulence was so short.

My experience was all about expectation management. I want you to anticipate difficulties so you can be prepared. Do not hope for things to be easy because you will only disappointed. You can handle anything, so be prepared for everything.

Do not get caught off guard when struggles show up or continue. Prepare for the hard and appreciate the easy.

4. Return It Better Than You Found It

The reflection of your integrity is found in how you leave things. When you leave a team, what do they say about you? Did you leave it better than you found it?

It is easy to become so self-centered that you fail to consider those following in your footsteps.

"Who cares how next year's team is! I will not be here!"

"The young players can figure it like I had to!"

Those are actual comments I often hear from veteran players. Failing to leave a legacy only guarantees that you leave scars. Those who follow you will talk about you, but never in a positive way.

You can leave the culture and team better by focusing on your effort, leading by example, treating everyone with respect, and accepting criticism in an open mind. Many eyes are watching how you handle the struggles and adversity. Show them you can leave the environment better, regardless of how you play.

5. Teach Another

Share your greatest lessons with others. You may think you are suffering, but someone else is likely struggling even more. Teach another about your experiences, and you will learn the most powerful lesson.

> You can teach another if you choose to see your experiences as beneficial, regardless of how difficult they are. There are lessons in your struggle, and when you are responsible for sharing those lessons with another, you will see them in a different light. Give your wisdom, and it will shine a light on your genius.

Your time is NOW. Stop seeing your potential as the target and focus on improving your skills, mindset, and perspective today.

19

MY FINAL WORD

This book was an evolution of my own Suckville experience. I battled the manuscript for a long time, but I never gave up on my vision for the content. The hardest part of the book was conveying a message that inspired hope instead of painting a picture of frustration and difficulty. It is so easy to see the negative side of things, even when writing a book.

Every single day, I meet clients who struggle to find the missing piece in their performance. From the top of the professional world through youth sports, the stories are similar – there has to be something missing in performance because the results seem to be less than I believe I can achieve. Their minds become the prison for their dreams and aspirations.

There have been or will be times in your performance journey where you will become imprisoned by your frustrations. It is a fact.

While it may feel insurmountable at times, many great things happen, but you overlook it because you get obsessed with frustration. Good and bad, success and failure are all around you, so it matters what you learn to focus on. The events in your life are beyond your control, but your thinking is always under your influence.

You own the right to see your future the way you want to. Are you a stock worth investing in or one that you would sell? It is all a matter of perception.

In thirty years, how will you look back at your journey? Will you see someone who gave all they had for the mere opportunity to succeed, or will you see someone who protected against mistakes? One of those will be filled with pride, and one will be filled with regret.

The Alumni Weekend

As I sat around the table, I listened to the war stories from my old teammates. I played with future Major League Baseball players, Olympians, and Hall of Famers, and listening to the variety of stories was enjoyable. Some of my teammates remained quiet and laughed, smiled, and cut up with each story.

Alumni weekends are some of my favorite reunions I get to go to each year. Although it has been over 25 years since our "glory days" on the field, it seems just like yesterday that each of us arrived from different parts of the country to compete together for a collective goal. Individual sacrifices had to be made by each team member, as those championships reflected purpose-driven mindsets and not a tally of those sacrifices. It is impressive to see how time washes away the emotional side of sacrifices and bonds a team around success.

In the present moment, it can be brutal to do what it takes to succeed, but after many years, those decisions seem intuitive and straightforward. The championships, memories, and friendships are worth it – for those who made the sacrifices.

There was another group sitting around the table. They were putting on a brave face, smiling and laughing just like everyone else, but they were hurting inside. Their memories were not as pleasurable.

One of those teammates pulled me to the side and asked me if their feelings of frustration and resentment were normal. I did not answer because I did not understand why they would feel that way, especially 25 years later.

"I hate the fact that I did not give everything when I was here. I felt like I was so frustrated by my lack of playing time, poor results, and uncertain future in the program that I never really went all-in. I was so pissed off when I finished up that I had a hard time talking about the baseball program for a long time. I felt like I had been wronged, and I could not let it go," my regretful teammate said.

I asked him, "Are you more upset that you could have been wronged or that you never gave everything you had?

Did you feel that you did not get a fair chance or that you did not perform with the opportunities you got?"

I know that question could be perceived as harsh, especially when he could not go back 25 years and change his attitude and effort. It was an important question, however.

"I am angry that I allowed my frustrations to keep me from figuring out how to crack the lineup and be a contributor in this program. I hate that I was just a part of the team." His sentiment hit me hard. I felt his pain and regret, yet there was nothing he could do about the past.

Regret continues to punish you long after the event has ended. It is unrelenting and causes emotional disarray for long periods. The memories will flood you at the most inconvenient times and hijack your focus from now and force you to live in the past.

You may not be able to undo the events of the past, but you can choose never to allow regret to enter your life again. I would never want to be like my teammate sitting at the table, regretting that he did not give all he had in college. His memories are not the same as those who did, even those who gave their all but failed. At least they gave all they had.

"If I could only go back and do it differently, my memories would be different," he lamented.

My answer to my teammate is the same recommendation I would make to you –

"It is up to you to define your future by how you see things right now." Just because you are frustrated about your past performances or your current progress, do not allow regret to define your attitude towards your future. Do not fall into the trap of bringing negativity forward. Remove it from your life and focus on your positive progress, opportunities, and that your reality is continuing to be a work in progress. It is up to you.

The way you see your future is the future you will create.

ABOUT THE AUTHOR

Dr. Bhrett McCabe is the founder of The MindSide, a center for Sports and Performance Psychology, and trusted advisor for the top performing competitors in the country. Dr. McCabe combines his personal experience as a 2x National Champion Division I athlete, his training as a licensed clinical psychologist, and his corporate leadership experience to help competitors achieve an elite performance mindset. Dr. McCabe develops personalized strategies and processes to help athletes and businesses achieve success at the highest levels. Dr. McCabe serves as the Sports & Performance Psychologist for elite-level athletes, corporate leaders, and teams including The University of Alabama Athletics, PGA Tour, NFL, and NBA. Dr. McCabe's strategies are also trusted by high-achieving businesses including multiple Fortune 500 organizations, Andrews Sports Medicine, and Titleist Performance Institute.

Dr. McCabe is the author of *The MindSide Manifesto: The Urgency to Create a Competitive Mindset* which he has developed to help athletes, coaches, and leaders compete to the best of their ability. Dr. McCabe also hosts a podcast, *The Secrets to Winning*, and has published several academic journal articles, presented numerous scientific presentations, as well as provided insight and authored articles for trade magazines such as GOLF Magazine, Golf World, Golf Week, and ESPNW, among others. Dr. McCabe has made several appearances on The Golf Channel's Morning Drive and The Golf Fix.

Dr. McCabe's latest endeavor is called Catalyst School, where Dr. McCabe provides weekly, live coaching sessions for anyone who is a catalyst for others - coaches and business leaders alike. More information can be found at www.bhrettmccabe.com/catalyst-school.

WHAT'S NEXT?

If you do not subscribe or listen already, check out Dr. McCabe's podcast, *The Secrets to Winning*, on Apple Podcasts, Spotify, or wherever you get your podcasts. You can also go to his website to view a full list of podcast episodes where Dr. McCabe interviews some of the most successful individuals in their competitive arena including world-class athletes, elite-level coaches, and the most brilliant minds in the business world.

bhrettmccabe.com/secrets-to-winning-podcast

If you are more of a visual person, Dr. McCabe's virtual training courses provide in-depth, game-changing strategies to improve your outcomes in whichever competitive arena you wish to excel.

bhrettmccabe.com/virtual-training

Dr. McCabe also has an extensive video library on YouTube consisting of his most in-depth discussions on mental performance and how you can continue to **Break Free From Suckville**.

YouTube.com/c/BhrettMcCabePhD

FOLLOW DR. McCABE ON SOCIAL MEDIA

@DRBHRETTMCCABE

Made in the USA
Columbia, SC
15 November 2021

48645552R00167